WAKE UP AND
SMELL THE COFFEE

WAKE UP AND SMELL THE COFFEE

365 Daily Doses of Reality

Andrew Frothingham
& Tripp Evans

BERKLEY BOOKS, NEW YORK

WAKE UP AND SMELL THE COFFEE

A Berkley Book / published by arrangement with
the authors

PRINTING HISTORY
Berkley trade paperback edition / December 1995

ISBN: 0-425-15135-2

BERKLEY®
Berkley Books are published by The Berkley Publishing Group,
200 Madison Avenue, New York, New York 10016.
BERKLEY and the "B" design
are trademarks belonging to Berkley Publishing Corporation.

PRINTED IN THE UNITED STATES OF AMERICA

10 9 8 7 6 5 4 3 2 1

To Patti and Lynn—
who wake up to the reality of us every morning

Introduction

Something deeply, tragically un-American is going on: people eager for understanding are being fed garbage. They seek wisdom, and they're offered nonsense about angelic inner children. Don't believe it (*see January 2—Your Inner Child Is a Brat*).

If these seekers had a family they loved and respected, they'd talk to a grandparent who'd tell them to "get a grip." Maybe they'd chat with an uncle who'd say, "Get with the program." Unfortunately, many of us have been told to ignore our family's wisdom by self-proclaimed, money-grabbing gurus offering up sets of fast-food, modern mantras called *affirmations* (*see April 24—People Who Talk About Self-Esteem Want Something From You*).

Like the affirmation books, we've broken our message down into convenient daily doses of reality. For each day of the year, there's a statement, a short meditation on that statement, and an action or realization to help you get through that particular day.

If you want the true serenity of knowing what you can't change, it's in this book. Start reading. It's time to *Wake Up and Smell the Coffee*.

JANUARY 1 ∽

YOU'RE HUNG OVER; YOU'RE PROBABLY AN ALCOHOLIC.

Shhh! Not so loud. You have a headache. We know, this is the last thing you want to deal with right now, especially after that great New Year's Eve. Quick: What did you do last night? Can't remember? Is it all kind of a blur? We thought so. Face it, you're a lush.

Throw this book in the corner, make yourself a Bloody Mary, and start our course of reality therapy tomorrow. (P.S. If you didn't touch a drop of booze last night, congratulations, you're a weenie.)

JANUARY 2 ∽

YOUR INNER CHILD IS A BRAT.

Can't you shut that kid up? "Buy me, give me, take me." You think you're the only one with an inner child whose needs have not been met? Well, think again. Our inner children need some attention, too, you big doody head.

Send your inner child to a military academy.

JANUARY 3 ∽

YOU WILL NEVER BE A ROCK STAR.

You may dream in your heart of hearts of being a rock star, but it's not going to happen. You are too settled in your life and too old. You wouldn't look good in spandex and you couldn't handle more than four groupies a night.

Accept it; buy an oldies record.

JANUARY 4 ∾

YOU AREN'T YOUR OWN BEST FRIEND.

Admit it. When was the last time you took yourself out to a really expensive candlelight dinner? How often have you looked at your naked body and actually liked what you saw? In reality, we all hate ourselves. We hate how we look, and we loathe having to spend extended periods of time alone.

Invite a friend to go to the movies with you. Try to ditch yourself.

JANUARY 5 ∞

YOU HAVE A LOT OF
EMOTIONAL "BAGGAGE."

Relationships are hard enough without baggage. But you come complete with all the wounds, complexes, habits, and defenses you've acquired as souvenirs of the past years. You'll never again have a shot at that moment when the two of you are the only people who matter in the world.

Go out with people with the same first name as your ex-love. That way, if you yell out the wrong name, it'll still be the right name.

JANUARY 6 ∞

LOOKS DO MATTER.

Inner beauty is fine, but . . .
Call up someone uglier than you.

JANUARY 7 ∽

TIME CAN'T BE MANAGED.

No matter what hyper, overdressed, manicured seminar leaders say, time can't be managed. It won't stop for you. You can't save seconds in a bank. No matter how neatly you fill in your personal organizer/calendar, you'll still get caught in traffic jams.

Keep reading this book. Everything else can wait.

JANUARY 8 ∽

YOU HAVE A BETTER CHANCE OF BEING HIT BY LIGHTNING THAN WINNING THE LOTTERY.

The odds of winning a lottery with a prize worth $12 million are about 1 in 34,475,684,284. The odds of being struck by lightning are 1 in 2,000,000. You figure it out.

Find some tall friends; if lightning strikes, they'll get hit first.

JANUARY 9 ∽

THE ODDS ARE YOU WERE A MISTAKE.

Birth control is a pretty iffy process. The odds are, you weren't planned. Your parents probably screamed and cursed when they found out you were on the way. They won't tell you this, but that's probably the way it was.

You lucked out; enjoy your life.

JANUARY 10 ∽

IF YOU ARE REALLY LIBERAL, YOUR KIDS WILL HAVE TO DO SOMETHING INSANELY DANGEROUS IN ORDER TO REBEL.

Go ahead: resolve not to be a strict disciplinarian like your parents were. Stay open to new ideas and new trends. That doesn't mean you and the kids will remain buddies. It just means that, in order to rebel, they'll either have to go far right and join the Nazi party, or go far, far, far left and join the Weather Underground.

Say, "No, because I'm the parent." Feels good, doesn't it?

JANUARY 11 ∽

YOU ARE BECOMING MORE AND MORE LIKE YOUR PARENTS.

Take a look in the mirror if you don't believe us. You're even starting to sound more and more like them.

Make yourself a martini.

7

JANUARY 12 ∽

YOU'VE FORGOTTEN EVERYTHING
YOU KNEW IN KINDERGARTEN.

Some nabob claims you can live your life on the lessons learned in kindergarten. Problem is, you've forgotten everything you learned back then.

Try eating stale graham crackers with warm milk. That might bring back a memory or two.

JANUARY 13 ∽

MAKING LISTS IS A SIGN
OF SERIOUS NEUROSIS.

Do you make lists? It may be a good way to organize things—or it may be the sign of a serious problem. Nuts make lists; it makes them feel like they have things under control.

Put "Stop Making Lists!" onto your list of "Things to Do."

JANUARY 14 ∾

LYING SEPARATES US FROM
OTHER ANIMALS.

When we met with the president of the United States, he asked us what we thought about this dose of reality. We quickly pointed out that lying is a creative process that tests one's true mettle. The bigger the lie, the greater the challenge to cover one's butt. Julia Roberts, my girlfriend at the time, laughed out loud when I mentioned "butt" in front of the president. Later, he and the First Lady took us for a ride in a UFO the Air Force captured in the Mojave Desert.

Go to the local zoo and tell the monkeys that the zookeeper just freed all the lions.

JANUARY 15 ∽

THE DAYS HAVE GOTTEN REALLY SHORT.

Scientists have discovered that the lack of sunlight in winter makes you suffer from depression and mood swings. It's at its worst about now. Look in the mirror. You look a little weepy, don't you—maybe a bit irrational. In your condition, you shouldn't operate heavy machinery or even be near your loved ones.

Book that Caribbean trip now.

JANUARY 16 ∽

BEING ENTHUSIASTIC CAN ONLY LEAD TO GREATER DISAPPOINTMENT.

Most efforts are bound to fail. High hopes and a positive attitude will only add to your misery and embarrassment.

Next time you feel an attack of enthusiasm coming on, take a Valium.

JANUARY 17 ∾

YOU'RE BEING NICE TO YOUR PARENTS BECAUSE THERE'S STUFF YOU WANT TO INHERIT—NOT BECAUSE YOU LOVE THEM.

Your parents are getting more and more crotchety, and you're getting nicer and nicer. Why? Because they have stuff you want and you're afraid they'll leave it all to a sibling, guru, or television evangelist.

Start taking notes so you can contest their will.

JANUARY 18 ∾

A COLLEGE DEGREE ISN'T WORTH THE PAPER IT'S WRITTEN ON.

Not only isn't it worth the paper it's written on, but you'll probably be in hock until it's time to retire. The cost of a college education is ridiculous, and it doesn't guarantee you a job.

When the alumni fund calls, ask *them* to give *you* money.

11

JANUARY 19 ∽

YOU ARE NO LONGER HIP.

You don't even know who the really hip groups are anymore. The stuff you like strikes kids as elevator music. Elastic waistbands are starting to make sense to you.

Take up golf.

JANUARY 20 ∽

THE PEOPLE WHO LAUGHED AT YOUR JOKES WERE PROBABLY HIGH.

You thought they were laughing hilariously at your witty bon mot. Forget about it. They were probably stoned and would have laughed uproariously even if you had read to them from an actuarial table.

Keep a box of Oreo cookies with you at all times.

JANUARY 21 ∞

THE SUPERBOWL IS JUST
A LOUSY FOOTBALL GAME.

It's been built up for months—the big game. But with so much on the line, the coaches are going to be conservative. There'll be more action in the ads than on the field. No matter how much brew you down, by the fourth quarter, it'll be clear that the announcers are desperately trying to convince you a meaningful battle is still going on.

Enter a box pool; that way you'll at least have a stake in the final score.

JANUARY 22 ∞

YOU'LL DO WHATEVER IT TAKES
TO AVOID RESPONSIBILITY.

I did not want to include this dose of reality in the book; it was my partner's idea.

Repeat after me: "It's not my job."

JANUARY 23 ∽

AS YOUR DAY GOES ON, THERE'S MORE OF A CHANCE THINGS ARE GOING TO GO WRONG.

Just think how many things can go wrong: your alarm doesn't go off, you sleep through it, there's no hot water, you burn the toast. And you haven't even gotten dressed yet.

Stay in bed.

JANUARY 24 ∽

YOUR COWORKERS ARE OUT TO DESTROY YOUR CAREER.

FYI, CYA ASAP. Translation: "For your information, cover your ass as soon as possible." Guardian angels don't stand a chance against the sharks of the business world—just ask Darwin.

Watch your back.

JANUARY 25 ∾

THE BRILLIANT IDEA THAT JUST HIT YOU IS PROBABLY REALLY DUMB.

You know what the odds are of ever having an original thought? Something like one in ten hundred billion trillion (don't quote us on that, but it's really, really high). Instead of wasting your time thinking of something clever to say and increasing your chances of showing off your ignorance, crib from the masters and claim their ideas as your own.

Buy a book of quotations (*And I Quote* is our favorite) and plagiarize liberally. Don't get caught.

JANUARY 26 ∞

PEOPLE DON'T REALLY CARE
WHAT YOU HAVE TO SAY.

Do you really believe people care what you have to say? This is a perfect example. We'll bet you thought about answering that question. Come on, admit it. On second thought, it doesn't really matter if you responded or not because we don't care.

Ask a friend a question and walk away in the middle of the answer.

JANUARY 27 ∞

YOU'RE SO VAIN, YOU PROBABLY THINK
THIS BOOK IS ABOUT YOU.

And you know, you're right. This book is really about you. If we can help just one person understand what it means to be a willing participant and understanding observer in this wondrous world of ours, then we've done our job. Our story is your story.

Buy more copies of this book and give them to your friends and family.

JANUARY 28 ∽

EVERYTHING YOU SAY CAN AND
WILL BE USED AGAINST YOU.

This is the exception to the rule (*see January 26—People Don't Really Care What You Have to Say*). If you admit your true, innermost feelings to others, prepare to have them thrown in your face on a later date. Just ask Miranda—it certainly wasn't his decision.

Watch an old cop show. Take notes.

JANUARY 29 ∽

IF YOU'RE OLDER THAN THIRTY,
YOUR LIFE HAS ALREADY PEAKED.

If you're not worrying about a mortgage, your kid's education, and your job, you're probably worrying about your rapidly decreasing marriage prospects, the rent on the home you'll never own, or your lack of proper health insurance coverage. What does all this mean? It means that with all this crap to worry about, you'll never get the time to test your true, creative potential.

If you have a job, call in sick. If you don't have a job, stay in bed for the day.

JANUARY 30 ∞

THE ODDS ARE VERY GOOD YOUR PARENTS WERE NOT VIRGINS WHEN THEY GOT MARRIED.

Think about it. They were teenagers once. They had hormones. And if they were just entering the Age of Aquarius or deep in the heart of the Sexual Revolution when they met, not only were they sleeping around, they were also dropping acid and smoking pot.

Have your DNA checked. You may have grounds for a lawsuit.

JANUARY 31 ∾

YOUR FRIENDS TALK ABOUT
YOU BEHIND YOUR BACK.

You're not paranoid. They **do** talk about your weight problem, your screwed-up marriage, and, if you're not married, what the chances are that you're gay.

Relax. It could be worse; they might not be talking about you at all.

FEBRUARY 1 ∾

GLASSES MAKE YOU LOOK SUSPICIOUS.

People like to see faces. They like eye contact. Glasses get in the way. What are you hiding, anyway?

Wear contacts.

FEBRUARY 2 ∾

A LOVED ONE IS DOING DRUGS
AND YOU DON'T KNOW IT.

Think all your friends are free from the scourge of drugs? The odds are you're wrong. One of them is addicted and hiding it from you. You don't know, so you can't help him. He'll just drift farther away from you.

Don't loan money to friends; you don't know what they'll do with it.

FEBRUARY 3 ∞

IF YOU THINK YOU'RE GOING TO SCREW UP THAT JOB INTERVIEW, YOU'RE PROBABLY RIGHT.

Your palms are wet, your clothes are drenched in sweat, your mind is a sieve, and you're **still** sitting in the waiting room. Well, guess what: this is probably the closest you're going to get to that job. We weren't made to face all this pressure. Unfortunately, potential employers know this and use it against us; their job is to make job hunting a living hell. Between the mind games, the competition, and the intimidation, you don't have a chance.

Go into business for yourself.

FEBRUARY 4 ∽

THINGS NEVER TURN OUT THE WAY
YOU'VE PLANNED.

All that time you spent trying to figure out how to
live your life was a waste. When was the last time
things went the way you hoped?

Take all your money out of savings and spend it
on lottery tickets.

FEBRUARY 5 ∽

YOU CAN'T BLAME EVERYTHING
ON YOUR PARENTS.

No matter how bad your childhood was, sooner or
later you have to take responsibility for yourself.
Some of the boneheaded things you do *are* your fault.

Disguise your voice, call your parents, and ask
them if their refrigerator is running. When they say
yes, tell them to go catch it. Hang up.

FEBRUARY 6 ∾

YOUR ACCOUNTANT HAS PROBABLY TOLD ALL HIS BUDDIES EXACTLY HOW LITTLE MONEY YOU HAVE—AND THEY'RE LAUGHING THEIR ASSES OFF.

In our great society, your income and finances define who you are and where you fit in the social schema. Your financial status can define how others see you. Unlike doctors, lawyers, and shrinks, accountants don't have to deal with the issue of confidentiality. Piss your accountant off and there's nothing to stop him or her from taking out a full-page ad in the local paper and reproducing your latest tax return. Talk about embarrassing.

Make a liberal cash contribution to your accountant's retirement fund. Don't worry; he or she should be able to write it off for you.

FEBRUARY 7 ✎

THERE'S NO SUCH THING AS HAPPINESS.

What is happiness, anyway? It's an amorphous, subjective state that's as ephemeral as quicksilver. Let's face it—one person's happiness could be your hell. We're happy you bought this book, but what if this book isn't what you expected and you're pissed off? One action, two different reactions. We don't know about you, but we're confused.

Buy another copy of the book for a friend. Make *us* happy.

FEBRUARY 8 ∾

CATS LOVE CAT HATERS.

Cats love cat haters because cat haters don't pick them up and talk baby talk to them as they cuddle, pet, and squeeze the life out of them. Cats particularly like people who are allergic to them because then they can rub up against their legs without being bothered.

Don't bother to pretend you like cats to keep them away; they can tell.

FEBRUARY 9 ∾

ACNE DOESN'T END WITH ADOLESCENCE.

No matter how old you are, you will get a zit the day you've planned to go on a date, scheduled a job interview, or been invited to an important social event. This is Nature's way of keeping you humble—as if you don't have enough problems.

Use your zit as a conversation icebreaker or as an effective visual aid, especially if you happen to be talking about volcanoes and how they work. Be creative.

FEBRUARY 10 ∾

YOUR THERAPIST WILL PROBABLY BE ON VACATION WHEN YOU NEED HIM OR HER MOST.

Unlike medical doctors, chiropractors, or massage therapists who provide definite, tangible relief, shrinks need a way to prove their importance. They can sense when their patients are close to a psychotic breakdown, and they plan their vacations accordingly. Many take a more proactive approach and plant seeds of doubt and insecurity around the last two weeks of July so they can get together with their buddies in August and talk about you.

If you can't beat 'em, join 'em. Rent *What About Bob?*

FEBRUARY 11 ∾

YOU ARE GOING TO DIE.

No way around it. You can't get away from it. You are going to die. You have no control over it. In the long run, you'll be ashes or worm food.

Don't floss tonight.

FEBRUARY 12 ∽

THERE'S NO SUCH THING AS
AN ACCIDENT.

Can't find your car keys? Just spilled a bowl of soup in your lap? Stepped on a stranger's foot while shopping at the mall? Think these are all accidents? Well, you're wrong. It's your subconscious working overtime. Face it, you really didn't want to get to work, the soup sucked, and if that butthead had looked where he was going, you wouldn't have had to teach him a lesson.

Next time, don't apologize, just say, "And that goes for the horse you rode in on, too!"

FEBRUARY 13 ✑

IT'S IN YOUR COWORKERS' BEST INTERESTS TO HAVE YOU FAIL.

Your coworkers are your team, your buddies, your pals; they'll watch your back for you, won't they? They are, if your company is expanding at the speed of light and everyone can get promoted at the same time. Otherwise, you stand in the way of their promotions, you hog their glory, and you might hold onto their slot when cutbacks come.

Keep files on their failures; they might come in handy.

FEBRUARY 14 ∽

YOUR "LOVED ONES" POSE A GREATER DANGER TO YOU THAN STRANGERS.

Worried about violence? Forget about ominous strangers. Better watch your spouse, parents, children, and lover, because statistics say they're the folks who are most likely to come after you with a kitchen knife.

Spread a box of cornflakes on the floor around your bed before you go to sleep so you can hear them coming.

FEBRUARY 15 ∽

NINE TIMES OUT OF TEN, YOUR INTUITION WILL GET YOU INTO DEEP TROUBLE.

How many times has that sixth sense of yours turned into nonsense? When are you going to learn that your perception of a situation is one tiny, insignificant frame of the bigger, grander movie?

Don't overexpose yourself; you'll just get hurt.

FEBRUARY 16 ∾

YOU'RE AS CREATIVE AS A STICK.

When was the last time you had a truly original thought? Take your time. Can't remember? We thought so. What you like to do is copy others' successes. Why not? Let the pioneer get in trouble while you reap the rewards.

Curl up on a futon with a cup of sake and a good book on Japanese business practices.

FEBRUARY 17 ∾

THE STUFF YOU LEARNED IN
SCHOOL IS MEANINGLESS.

You spent years of your life studying stuff that has since been revised. You will never need to know the French word for lamp shade, you will never have to name the planets in correct order, and it doesn't matter that you can name the first ten presidents.

Buy Trivial Pursuit or play along with *Jeopardy*.

FEBRUARY 18 ∽

IF YOU THINK YOUR MATE IS CHEATING ON YOU, YOU'RE PROBABLY RIGHT.

Take a look at the clock. If your mate isn't with you, do you know where he or she is? If he or she told you, do you really believe him or her? Go ahead, make a phone call, check it out. We'll wait. What?! You believed him or her? He or she is lying. Face it, you're always the last to know. Sorry if we ruined your day, but we couldn't just sit by and watch you get hurt. You'll thank us once you stop feeling the pain.

Call your mother.

FEBRUARY 19 ✑

HUMANS ARE TERRITORIAL.

Cooperation rarely works. Everyone wants to protect his or her own turf. No one will like your ideas. People in families you marry into will resent you. Join a company and the people already there will despise you.

Mark your territory. As you travel, use as many bathrooms as possible.

FEBRUARY 20 ∽

THE GOVERNMENT KNOWS MORE ABOUT
YOUR PRIVATE LIFE THAN
YOUR MOTHER DOES.

Have a Social Security number? A driver's license? A mortgage? How about a passport or a car loan? Remember filling out those pesky applications and the questions they asked you? Well, if you don't, Uncle Sam and his little computer certainly do. Step out of line and watch how fast they zap your credit information to every collection agency in the country. Big Brother is watching, and you can't do a damn thing about it.

Pay cash or barter only.

FEBRUARY 21 ∽

IF YOU WANT SOMETHING BADLY ENOUGH, YOU'LL DO WHATEVER IT TAKES TO GET IT.

Ever compromise your standards? Stretched the truth? Stepped on a few friends? Face it, you're a whore (*see September 7—You're a Whore*).

Make a list of everything you want. Then tell yourself you deserve it—in fact, you *need* it.

FEBRUARY 22 ∾

> **IF YOU'RE A SINGLE, HETEROSEXUAL
> FEMALE, 35 YEARS OR OLDER, YOU HAVE A
> BETTER CHANCE OF BEING CAPTURED BY
> ALIENS THAN GETTING MARRIED.**

And that's a fact—especially in urban areas. Not only is there a dearth of single, heterosexual males, those who are ready to settle down are looking for younger women who haven't begun to feel the pinch of gravity and crow's feet.

Treat yourself to a makeover. At least your female friends will appreciate it.

FEBRUARY 23 ∽

YOU DIDN'T WRITE THIS BOOK.

You've thought everything in this book at one time or another. But it never occurred to you to write it all down and organize it. You could have been the author and gotten paid for your cynicism, but we beat you to it.

Buy some canvas, throw a couple of buckets of paint on it. We've got the "author" angle covered, you can be the "modern artist."

FEBRUARY 24 ∽

YOUR MISSION IS TO JUDGE OTHERS.

That's right. How else are you going to know where you stand? Judging people helps build one's self-esteem; it allows you to demonstrate how much better, smarter, and wiser you are than that idiotic friend of yours who dirties a spoon because he put the sugar in *after* pouring the coffee instead of before.

Practice shaking your head slowly in front of a mirror as you breathe a deep sigh of frustration.

FEBRUARY 25 ❧

YOU ARE BEING JUDGED BY
EVERYONE YOU KNOW.

How else are your friends going to feel superior? Your friends secretly mock what you're wearing, what you do for a living, who you're seeing, where you live, what you eat, how you talk, walk, sit . . . That's why they're your friends; you give them a reason for living because, compared to you, they're doing very well.

Hire a public relations firm.

FEBRUARY 26 ❧

YOUR MATE FINDS YOU ABOUT AS
EXCITING AS YOU FIND HIM OR HER.

Is your significant other starting to seem a little less surprising and exotic? Do you like him, her, or it better with clothes on than naked? Are you living vicariously through your single friends?

Surprise your mate; cover your body in Saran Wrap.

FEBRUARY 27 ∽

YOUR SHIT STINKS.

Reality check. You're human. Your body takes in all of the pesto, sushi, Big Macs, and Devil Dogs and turns them into steaming, seething, stinking turds.

Buy an air freshener.

FEBRUARY 28 ∽

IF YOU WEREN'T SUCH A WIMP, YOU'D PROBABLY BE A BULLY.

You turn the other cheek because it's better to get the beating over with than prolong the pain. Pretty much the way you live, isn't it? Grin and bear it, because there's nothing you can do. Why? Because you're a wimp. "The meek shall inherit the earth"— not in your lifetime. What would happen if suddenly you were capable of beating the crap out of people? You'd love it. And why not? It's your turn. You deserve it—you wimp.

Buy an ant farm and make yourself their leader.

FEBRUARY 29 ∽

WE HAVE A SCREWED UP CALENDAR.

The calendar that rules our lives is a disaster. February is short, but Augustus Caesar (August) and Julius Caesar (July) both had to have long months named after them. And February 29 only shows up every four years like some strange comet. There are fixed holidays, like July 4, and religious holidays like Easter or Chanukah that float around.

Find a priest and ask him how Christ's birth can stay fixed on one day, but his death date keeps changing.

MARCH 1 ∾

WHEN YOU MAKE LOVE TO SOMEONE, HE OR SHE IS PROBABLY FANTASIZING ABOUT SOMEONE ELSE.

There it is—that peak of passion when your lover's eyes are clenched shut. It may be the agony of ecstasy; but the odds are there are mental movies playing on the inside of the eyelids.

Tape some erotic art to the ceiling.

MARCH 2 ∾

YOU AREN'T NEARLY AS COOL AS YOU THINK YOU ARE.

You tried drinking booze, smoking cigarettes, and doing illicit drugs to be cool, but that doesn't work. You can't pull off the macho thing, and you're not sensitive enough to handle the New Age rubbish. Face the facts: some people have it; you don't.

Buy a pocket protector, take a computer course, and put tape on your glasses. There'll always be a place for nerds.

MARCH 3 ∞

YOU CALL OTHER PEOPLE MORE
THAN THEY CALL YOU.

Sure, you have a great social life. But what would happen if you stopped doing all the calling and organizing? You'd be picking up the phone every few days just to see if it was still working.

Stop flattering yourself; get rid of call waiting.

MARCH 4 ∞

LIVE ONE DAY AT A TIME AND
YOU'LL STARVE.

Remember the fable about the ant and the grasshopper? Or was it the ant and the cockroach? Whatever. One of the insects saved up food for the winter while the other hung out and took life a day at a time. Something happened around wintertime when there wasn't a lot of food available . . . you get the picture.

Buy canned goods and put some money in an IRA.

MARCH 5 ∞

YOUR "FRIENDS" HAVE NO CLUE
AS TO WHO YOU REALLY ARE.

Look at the gifts you've gotten from your friends. Childish. Tasteless. And, when it comes to that alligator lamp, just plain bizarre. They have no idea what you like. Perhaps they just don't care.

Start your autobiography; try to fit the word *painful* in the title.

MARCH 6 ∞

YOU'LL FALL INTO THE SAME TRAP TWICE.

Ain't that the truth. How many people do you know who are on their second marriages?

Don't sign anything until you read the small print.

MARCH 7 ∽

EVEN IF YOU NEVER DRINK ANOTHER DROP, YOUR KID WILL STILL JOIN ADULT CHILDREN OF ALCOHOLICS SOMEDAY.

You could be a complete teetotaler, but even that won't save you. They'll say you had alcoholic patterns left over from your great-great-great grandfather. Everything that goes wrong in your kid's life will be your fault.

Take embarrassing naked pictures of the kid now. You'll need them as bargaining chips.

MARCH 8 ∞

YOU'LL PROBABLY NEVER BE ABLE TO
AFFORD A HOME OF YOUR OWN.

Gone are the days of the $15,000 starter homes your parents could afford. Today, $15,000 might just get you a car with a cramped backseat or it might be a down payment on a 500-square-foot studio apartment in a not-very-good section of some big city or for about $15,000 you can buy a log cabin kit and erect it in the middle of some godforsaken, backwater wilderness in the bowels of North Dakota. Any way you slice it, a nice little home in suburbia is probably not in your cards. Well, at least not in this life.

Be *really* nice to your parents.

MARCH 9 ∽

MEMOS ARE MEANINGLESS.

Your memos may be great: short, concise, clear, copied to all the right people, and even actionable. But they're still just memos: fancy ways of covering your ass and allocating blame. And half the time they can be used against you.

Stop writing memos, but save every one you get as possible evidence.

MARCH 10 ∽

DENIAL IS A GREAT COPING MECHANISM.

Denial is a wonderful defense, and you use it more often than you'd admit.

If anyone asks, deny you ever read this.

MARCH 11 ∞

HEELS MAKE YOU LOOK
AWKWARD, NOT TALLER.

Remember when you were a kid and you thought that when you grew up, you'd automatically know how to walk in heels? Wrong! The only kind of guy who's really turned on by your wobble is a chiropractor.

Wear Birkenstocks.

MARCH 12 ∞

YOU HAVE NO RHYTHM.

You can't dance and you can't carry a tune, yet you continue to force your friends to go out dancing with you. It's embarrassing. What are you trying to prove? If you must dance, do it in the privacy of your own home. Lock the door and pull down the blinds. Epileptics have better rhythm than you.

Stare at a rapidly blinking light and go with the flow.

MARCH 13 ∞

IF YOU WAKE UP NEXT TO SOMEONE
YOU DON'T KNOW, IT'S PROBABLY
THE RESULT OF ALZHEIMER'S.

Double whammy! Your days of catting around are over and you're getting older. You don't have the looks, technique, or even the desire needed to have one-night stands. But life still has surprises in store. The person you've been married to for years will someday seem as fresh and unusual as ever before—you'll have forgotten both of your names.

Call everyone either "ma'am" or "sir;" they'll think you're young and polite.

MARCH 14 ∞

WHEN YOU THINK YOU'RE BEING FUNNY, EVERYONE ELSE SEES YOU AS PATHETIC.

There's a fine line between people laughing with you and laughing at you; one is good, the other is bad. Can you tell the difference? You probably can't because you're so hungry for attention—any kind of attention—that any impartial awareness you once had has flown out the proverbial window. In fact, we're laughing at you right now.

Cut this page out and fax it to a friend. Buy a new copy of the book so you still have a complete one.

MARCH 15 ∞

YOU BORE YOUR THERAPIST.

Many people suffered real trauma as they grew up, but the only things battered during your childhood were fish sticks and french toast.

Skip a session so you'll have something to feel guilty about.

MARCH 16 ∾

YOU CAN'T STOP NEPOTISM.

Blood is thicker than water, and the only thing thicker than blood is the boss's son, who will be working in your department until he's ready to take your job. No matter how many rules you make, families will find ways to take care of their own. If the company can't hire the CEO's daughter, surely the ad agency can. And the senator's younger brother will somehow manage to get his building projects approved.

Tell the boss's son the work you have for him is demeaning; transfer him to an enemy's department.

MARCH 17 ∾

THE STUFF IN YOUR CLOSET WILL
NEVER COME BACK INTO STYLE.

Even if it did, you could never fit into it.
Throw it out.

MARCH 18 ∽

RUNNING AWAY IS THE SAFEST COURSE.

Why stick around and get blasted for possibly doing something you shouldn't have when you could easily turn tail and split? Go with your gut. If you're not sure if you're guilty or not, don't stay to find out. If you are guilty, by the time the injured party finds you, enough time should have elapsed so you won't get in the kind of trouble you may have if you were caught red-handed.

Buy yourself an extra pair of sneakers.

MARCH 19 ✑

BY THE TIME YOU'RE OLD ENOUGH TO AFFORD THE LUXURY OF A REALLY FAST SPORTS CAR, YOUR REFLEXES WILL BE TOO SLOW.

If you got a really hot car now, the kids on the corner wouldn't look at you in awe and think, "cool," they'd think, "midlife crisis." Besides, what you really should get is one of those safe, boxy sedans—or, maybe a station wagon. Better still, hold on to the old car until the kids have learned to drive.

Go to an amusement park—ride the bumper cars.

MARCH 20 ✑

YOU THINK TOO MUCH.

Try spontaneity.
Do it.

MARCH 21 ∽

YOUR MOTHER-IN-LAW WILL NEVER, EVER APPRECIATE YOU.

Come on, you've taken her baby from her. To add insult to injury, you're also having sex with her sweet, little darling. She's done all the work while you reap the benefits. Do you really think she's going to give up without a fight?

During those awkward visits, tell her some tasteless mother-in-law jokes to help break the ice.

MARCH 22 ∞

YOUR ANSWERING MACHINE
MESSAGE STINKS.

"No one is home right now to answer your call . . ."
Great! Tell me something I don't know. The only
person that information benefits is the local burglar
who you just tipped off that it's safe to rob you blind.
How about, "I'm sorry, I can't come to the phone
right now . . ."? Another winner. Finally, all those
"creative" messages or messages accompanied by music tell everyone you have too much free time, and
get boring and annoying really fast.

Rerecord your message. Just leave your number and
be done with it.

MARCH 23 ∽

REMEMBER THE TEN POUNDS YOU MADE A NEW YEAR'S RESOLUTION TO LOSE? THEY'RE STILL THERE AND THEY'VE GOT FRIENDS.

You finally psyched yourself up for the big diet. You had the exercise plan all worked out. And it worked—for three days of water loss. But other priorities—and pounds—came along.

Chase a Good Humor truck.

MARCH 24 ∽

CHILDBEARING WILL ALWAYS BE WOMAN'S WORK.

Sorry about that, but it's the luck of the draw. A woman can have kids, a man can't. It's that simple. Accept the fact and go on with your life. Now, stop complaining and get supper ready.

Get supper ready.

MARCH 25 ∽

LOVE TAKES TOO MUCH WORK.

What a pain in the butt. Remember to call, write, send an E-mail message. Don't forget the birthday, anniversary, Saint Valentine's Day. Keep a comprehensive list of gifts given, names, and relevant information about your lover's family and foods liked and disliked. No matter how comprehensive you are, you're going to neglect something. And that minor transgression will erase years of good behavior.

Buy a notebook computer and create a database.

MARCH 26 ∽

IF THE FASHION POLICE REALLY EXISTED,
YOU'D BE SERVING A LIFE SENTENCE.

You just don't get it, do you? Stripes and plaids don't go together. You have the choice to wear what you wish, but you must understand that others have to look at you. By all means, make your own individual fashion statement, but please think of those around you. There ought to be a law.

Buy everything in black. Saves money on dry cleaning, too.

MARCH 27 ∽

THE OSCARS ARE BORING.

If you're not in the film industry and you're able to sit through three and a half tedious hours of Oscar programming, you deserve an Oscar for Most in Need of a Life. Who cares about Best Film Editor, Best Costume, or Best Sound Mix, other than film editors, costume designers, and sound technicians? And those music productions are insufferable—elevator Muzak is more entertaining.

Pretend you're a fashion critic; rate everyone on their outfits.

MARCH 28 ∽

POLICE WHO STOP YOU ARE LIKELY TO RESENT YOU FOR MAKING MORE THAN THEY DO.

Speeding is no big crime. But the cop who stops you may be having a bad day. He gets shot at on the job, while the worst thing that's likely to happen to you is a bad performance review—but your car is a lot nicer than his secondhand Nova. It may not be probable cause, but at the moment, you're a probeable suspect.

Fielder's choice: Join the ACLU or put a Police Athletic League sticker in the rear window.

MARCH 29 ∞

ONLY THE LEAD SLED DOG HAS
A GOOD VIEW.

The leaders, the ones out front, get to see what's really happening; they get to see the panorama of nature go by. For the rest of us, the view is a bit different.

Continue to follow—the lead dog also falls through the ice first.

MARCH 30 ∞

SOME DOCTORS GO INTO
MEDICINE BECAUSE IT'S A
GOOD WAY TO MAKE MONEY.

If your doctor was really concerned with the good of mankind, he or she would be off in a Third World country treating epidemics. Instead, the good doctor is concentrating on alleviating obesity in your bank account.

Develop a really good golf game so you can win some of your money back.

MARCH 31 ∽

COPYING ISN'T JUST THE HIGHEST FORM OF FLATTERY; IT'S SAFER.

Just ask Hollywood, big business, or the publishing world: stealing others' ideas is the way to go. When in doubt, copy the plot line of a blockbuster movie, come out with a me-too product, or write a book on the same topic as a current best-seller. It's all fair game. In fact, you shouldn't consider it as copying (or plagiarism or stealing), but as your way of showing your appreciation of a job well done. If their concept had failed, you wouldn't have gone anywhere near it.

Get subscriptions to *Variety*, *New York Times Book Review*, and *Forbes*.

APRIL 1 ∽

YOU AND YOUR FRIENDS AREN'T CREATIVE ENOUGH TO COME UP WITH ANY DECENT APRIL FOOL'S PRANKS.

April Fools' Day is a wonderful tradition. Biographies of the great always include tales of inventive but essentially gentle hoaxes that they played. But you've lost that youthful spirit. All you can think of was stupid tricks from your childhood. Besides, you're too busy.

Tape a "Kick Me" sign to someone's back.

APRIL 2 ∽

EACH COUNTRY GETS THE GOVERNMENT IT DESERVES.

This isn't a new thought, but ponder its implications. The people in Washington who run the government would as soon lie as breathe. They feel no obligation to tell the truth. That's what we deserve? What an indictment.

Be happy you're not in Bosnia.

APRIL 3 ∽

IT'S EASIER TO FAIL THAN TO SUCCEED.

This isn't really news to you, is it? Your failures far outweigh your successes. But take heart, you're not avoiding success or even afraid of it; you're just incapable of it. Relax and enjoy where you are. You're not alone, and misery loves company.

Call a fellow loser and complain about your awful job, a failed relationship, or your alcoholic parents.

APRIL 4 ∽

IF ANGELS EXISTED, THEY'D BE CONSIDERED BIG GAME.

Angels are overrated. If there were a bunch of innocent angels flying around, there'd be a bunch of maniacs hunting them and hanging their wings over their fireplaces. It's probably a good thing angels don't exist. They'd ruin your car's front end and break their necks flying into your picture windows.

Next time someone mentions angels, ask them where angel dust comes from.

APRIL 5 ∽

YOUR BOSS WILL NEVER BE SATISFIED, JUST THREATENED.

Your boss is only human. He or she is as paranoid, distrustful, and intimidated as the next person. Why should she think your motives are altruistic? We all know we're out to get whatever we can in this life. And your boss knows she has to watch out that you don't try to make her look bad by making yourself look good.

Stay home from work, mess up that big deal, or misplace the slides for the next business meeting. Your boss will thank you in her own unique way.

APRIL 6 ∞

SOCIETY MAKES US WISH FOR
UNATTAINABLE BODIES.

Our society's view of the perfect body shape is absurd. You'll only look like that in your dreams and you know it. So do something about it. Instead of sitting through advertisements showing off tall, thin, leggy women or small-waisted, broad-shouldered men with washboard stomachs, you should complain to the advertisers of the world and force them to use real people in their ads—people like us. Let's celebrate our beer guts, flat feet, bald pates, thick thighs, tiny boobs, and fat butts. Power to the couch potato!

To hell with the diet; eat a box of Fig Newtons.

APRIL 7 ∞

THE WORLD IS DYING.

The pollution of the industrial era is leaking out and destroying the environment. The rain forests are going. The seas are sewers. And the sun will burn you into a tumor.

Study astronomy—you may live up there someday.

APRIL 8 ∞

THE BOOKS THAT INSPIRED YOU ARE SIMPLE, CRASS, AND DUMB.

Remember the books that really made you cry? *Love Story, Jonathan Livingston Seagull, The Bridges of Madison County, Standing Firm?* Look at them again. Monkeys would have been embarrassed to write such hogwash.

Read a Harlequin Romance. It's hogwash, too; but it's honest hogwash.

APRIL 9 ∽

MOST PEOPLE WHO CALL YOU
BY YOUR FIRST NAME
WANT SOMETHING FROM YOU.

It may seem like you've got a lot of friends, but who would you talk to if you really had a problem? The people who call you by your first name are probably trying to sell you something.

Next time you meet someone for the first time, use his or her first name a lot, the way salesmen do. Watch the person back away.

APRIL 10 ∞

OUR BODIES WEREN'T DESIGNED TO LAST PAST THE AGE OF 45.

Our bodies were designed for life on the prehistoric plains. They have great adrenaline pumps that provide us with the energy for fight or flight. They store fat so we can make it through hard times. But they were only designed to last for forty-five years or so. After that, we're just patching things with metal joints, dental bridges, contact lenses, and hearing aids—not to mention laxatives, pacemakers, and various prosthetic gizmos.

Enjoy the advantages of aging: you can be crabby as hell and get away with it.

APRIL 11 ∽

SIZE REALLY DOES MATTER.

Whoever coined, "It's not the pen, it's the penmanship," had a small penis and hoped to detract from his inadequacy with that silly little metaphor. No matter what anyone says, size *does* matter, and don't you forget it. Stop grinning, girls—this counts for boobs, too.

Do tongue exercises—you'll have to compensate somehow.

APRIL 12 ∽

YOU HAVE NO WILLPOWER.

How many diets have you been on? How many times have you tried to quit smoking, cut down on your drinking, get more exercise, watch less TV, read more, write more . . . ? The list goes on and on and you've let yourself down on more than hundreds of occasions. What are you, a masochist or something? Willpower is just a control issue, anyway.

Go with the flow—pig out.

APRIL 13 ∽

THERE IS NO CURE FOR HAT HEAD.

No one can get away with hat hair. Between the matted-down tufts of hair and the static electricity, at best you look like you just got out of bed; at worst you look like a relative of Forrest Gump. People will laugh at you and no one will take you seriously.

Shave all your hair off, only wear ear muffs, or tough it out. Fashion rules.

APRIL 14 ∽

IF YOU WERE REALLY SENSITIVE, YOU'D COMMIT SUICIDE.

You're a S.N.A.P.: Sensitive New Age Person. You recycle. You care deeply about whales, and have sworn never to eat blubber. But, face it, if you really, really felt the world's woes, you'd be overwhelmed and kill yourself.

Go bowling.

APRIL 15 ∽

TAX FORMS WERE DESIGNED
TO BE UNDERSTANDABLE BY A
FIFTH GRADER . . . AND YOU CAN'T
HANDLE THEM.

Everyone has to pay taxes. Not just brain surgeons, but also the guy at the gas station who has trouble working the register. And the tax forms were designed so all citizens can handle them. But you find them bewildering and terrifying. What's wrong with this picture?

Put all of your receipts into folders. It won't help you with the forms, but it makes things look neater.

APRIL 16 ∞

YOUR ORGAN DONOR CARD GIVES
MEDICAL TECHNICIANS AN INCENTIVE TO
LET YOU DIE.

Sure, carrying an organ donor card is the right thing to do, but think of it from the point of view of the medical technician. You're almost, basically, sort of a goner, but your parts could give that cute girl in Room 1218 another chance at life. Besides, the operation will make headlines in the local paper.

Reread *Coma*.

APRIL 17 ∞

YOU WILL NEVER WRITE
THE GREAT AMERICAN NOVEL.

The classics are overrated. The books that are considered classics are long, boring, and generally irrelevant. If they were written today, they wouldn't get published.

Watch more TV.

APRIL 18 ∞

CLERKS CALL YOU "SIR" OR "MA'AM."

Think you're still one of the young set? Listen to what they're calling you: ma'am and sir. You're respected . . . and old.

Report the young whippersnappers to the manager; complain of harassment.

APRIL 19 ∞

YOUR SHIP IS NEVER COMING IN—IT SANK OFF THE CAPE OF GOOD HOPE.

Stop with all those fish stories; it's not going to happen. The turbulent waters of life are rife with razor-sharp reefs of reality whose sole purpose is to puncture, rend, and cleave your paper-thin boat of dreams to shark bait. And if, by some fluke of nature, your ship manages to maneuver those treacherous shoals and frothy waters, the cargo won't be what you expected—just ask the crew of the *Flying Dutchman*.

Take a nice long bubble bath.

APRIL 20 ∾

YOU HAVEN'T SUFFERED ANY REAL DEPRIVATION, SO YOU WILL NEVER BE A GREAT ARTIST.

Braces in seventh grade, the horrible haircut your sister gave you, the terrible two-week crush on the riding teacher, and the inability to climb the rope in gym may have all been painful at the time, but they don't add up to real dues. They're nothing like chopping your ear off. True artists really suffer.

Consider being a collector.

APRIL 21 ∞

YOU ARE NOT AS SPECIAL AS YOU THINK.

You get up in the morning and you peer back at that face in the mirror and you think, "Look out world, here I come!" You're ready to face the day. Well, look around you. Over a million people are doing the exact same thing as you. Unfortunately, only a handful—at best—will achieve the greatness they think they deserve. Are you one of them? Don't let it get you down. You're not alone.

Watch a *special* on TV. Send something *special* delivery. Go out to lunch and order the *special*.

APRIL 22 ∾

IN A PREVIOUS LIFE, YOU WERE A PEASANT.

Believe in reincarnation if you must, but accept the fact that you weren't Napoleon or Cleopatra. Those antecedents have already been claimed. The chances are good that you were a weasel, an earwig, or a newt. And if you were human, you were probably a serf, vassal, or peasant.

Start your regressive research. If you lie down when you sleep, you were probably a snake.

APRIL 23 ∾

IF YOU PLANT A TREE,
ACID RAIN WILL KILL IT.

The world is delicately balanced between humans who use oxygen and plants that emit oxygen. But now we've managed to poison the system to the extent that it kills trees. It's kind of like one Siamese twin shooting the other.

Hug a tree; then be sure to wash.

APRIL 24 ∽

PEOPLE WHO TALK ABOUT SELF-ESTEEM
WANT SOMETHING FROM YOU.

The self-esteem movement has trained more swindlers than Dickens's Fagin. Next time someone starts babbling about self-esteem, put both hands on your wallet and hold tight. Charlatans love the self-esteem movement, because self-esteem can't be measured, and therefore you can't prove them wrong.

Pretend you're hard of hearing. Whenever they say "issues," hand them a box of tissues.

APRIL 25 ∞

YOUR CHILDREN WILL NEVER MOVE OUT.

And if they have, be prepared for them to move back any day now. Cutbacks, layoffs, hiring freezes, and downsizing add up to the continued patter of little feet as your kids' kids mess up your chance for the quiet, contemplative life that's supposed to come with old age.

Add a wing on the dog house for you and your spouse.

APRIL 26 ∞

NO ONE WILL TELL YOU HOW TO GET RICH.

If they really knew how, they'd keep it to themselves. And they wouldn't have to make videos, send out mailers, or give seminars. Tip one for how to get rich: Don't waste your money on get-rich programs.

Buy a lottery ticket. The odds are preposterous, but at least you don't have to make lists of your strengths and weaknesses or visualize anything.

APRIL 27 ∽

THE RULES KEEP CHANGING.

Understand the rules of cricket, that silly game the Brits play? Neither do we, which is why it's a perfect metaphor for life. Running back and forth between two posts, playing without mitts, knocking some sticks over, and hitting the ball with something that looks like a fraternity pledge paddle—we give up. None of it makes any sense, and that's our point.

Challenge a six-year-old to a game of Scrabble. Trounce him or her soundly.

APRIL 28 ∽

YOU DON'T HAVE BAD LUCK—YOU MAKE BAD CHOICES.

Bad luck with that marriage? And the car? And the job? No such luck. They were all decisions you made—bad ones. If you get hit by a meteor, that's bad luck. But own up to the rest of it.

Throw out the Saint Christopher's medal—he's been demoted, anyway.

APRIL 29 ∽

YOUR SEX LIFE IS BORING.

When was the last time you and your loved one rented a porno video, covered your body in whipped cream, or slapped on the handcuffs? The odds are good you're the once-a-week, he's-on-top, only-perverts-really-enjoy-sex, it's-more-like-a-job kind of folk.

All you men, get into your secret stash of porno magazines and share them with your mate; and you women, introduce your vibrator to your spouse. See what, if anything, develops.

APRIL 30 ∽

YOU ARE BLOWING YOUR CHANCE
TO MAKE A MILLION.

Not only did your grandparents not make the one investment that would have put you on easy street, right now you're missing the one that would set up your grandchildren for life. They will never forgive you.

Play monopoly and bequeath Park Place to your children.

MAY 1 ∾

YOUR NEIGHBOR'S KID IS
SMARTER THAN YOURS.

You've done everything you could, but it's not going to happen; your kid just doesn't have it. The teachers tried to tell you, the tests tried to tell you, but you just wouldn't listen; your child is average. Forget Ivy League, Seven Sisters, PAC 10, and the rest. Focus on someplace your kid's going to get into, like a community college, trade school, or vocational institution.

Don't spend the little money you may have already set aside for the kid's college. You may need it for bail money.

MAY 2 ∽

MEN AND WOMEN ARE ON
DIFFERENT SEXUAL SCHEDULES.

Males reach their sexual peak in their teens, while women in their teens are looking for older, richer men. Females reach their peak in their thirties, when the men are looking for younger, smoother women. It doesn't work. We weren't made for each other.

Lie about your age.

MAY 3 ∽

YOU'LL NEVER KNOW WHETHER OR NOT
YOUR MOTHER REALLY LOVED YOU.

Your mother may just have been doing her job. Of course, if you ask her if she really loves you, she'll say, "Yes"—that's part of the job.

Add a box of chocolates to the obligatory Mother's Day card. Sleep with one eye open.

MAY 4 ∽

THE ECONOMIC SAFETY NET
HAS A MAJOR HOLE IN IT.

It's not there for you. Sure, you could get unemployment—if you had a regular job to start with. And Social Security might help, if you're a hopeless drunk or an addict. And welfare is there, at a pittance a month, once you've sold the house and car. And to get any of this, you'll have to get past a wall of bureaucrats who make the post office seem efficient.

Befriend a politician. They always seem to retire rich.

MAY 5 ∽

REALITY BITES.

Enough said.
Don't get out of bed for the next three days.

MAY 6 ∽

ALL THE GOOD WARS ARE OVER.

Read Virgil, Homer, and Shakespeare. They'll all tell you that the true test of a man is war. But all the good wars are over. Vietnam and Korea were embarrassing, pointless political disasters. Dream of Sergeant York and Ivanhoe all you want, but there'll never be another war that seems glorious; from here on out, they're all nasty, bureaucratic charades.

Make love.

MAY 7 ∽

YOUR SHRINK HAS MORE
PROBLEMS THAN YOU DO.

Anybody and his mother can hang out a shingle and call him- or herself a psychotherapist. Pretty scary, huh? Ever thought about what attracts people to this profession? How about a God complex mixed with an aversion to blood? Or maybe having a life that's so messed up it's easier to "help" others than work on their own issues?

Think twice if your shrink asks you to lie down on the couch.

MAY 8 ∽

YOUR MEMORY IS GOING.

It's not dynamic blocking of traumatic events; it's old age. Quick: What words of wisdom did we offer you two days ago? The knees are next.

Positive reinforcement test: Recite the alphabet.

MAY 9 ∞

YOUR EATING HABITS SUCK.

And it shows. Your face is breaking out constantly, and your stomach and thighs have their own zip codes. Clearly you don't consider your body a temple—or maybe you do. The Temple of Doom perhaps?

Invest in PepsiCo—they own Frito-Lay, too.

MAY 10 ∞

YOUR TEETH ARE DECAYING.

Remember how gross it was when Grandpa took out his choppers? It's happening to you, too. No matter how much you brush, your teeth are wearing down. You are going to outlive them. Face it, your golden years are going to be spent at the dentist where he will fit and refit those unwieldy, painful, ill-fitting dentures.

Eat an apple, while you still can.

MAY 11 ∞

YOUR DENTIST ENJOYS INFLICTING PAIN.

Why else would he or she pick this sadomasochistic profession? Dentists do the same thing over and over. After filling thousands and thousands of cavities and performing hundreds of root canals, they must get bored. How different can one mouth be from another? Eventually, they discover that their lives are one huge gaping maw and they're angry. They've gotten used to a lifestyle and the shallow prestige that goes along with being a "doctor" and they're stuck. So why not stick it to you?

Rent *Marathon Man*. Buy a new toothbrush.

MAY 12 ∽

YOU'LL NEVER BE RICHER
THAN YOUR PARENTS.

Look at those old photos of your parents. The reason they look so smug is that they were way ahead of their parents. But not you. You're downwardly mobile. Not only will you never be ahead of your parents, you'll probably have to borrow from them, or maybe even live with them.

Sell the family silver.

MAY 13 ∽

QUICK, WHEN WAS THE LAST TIME YOU USED YOUR EXPENSIVE EXERCISE MACHINE?

Where is it? Under your bed gathering dust? Rusting quietly in the closet? Acting as a second clothes rack? You bought it because it was the thing to do and you felt out of shape and guilty. You bought it, but you haven't touched it, and guess what, you're still overweight.

Get rid of the damn thing—maybe you'll lose some weight in the process.

MAY 14 ∞

MOTHER'S DAY IS A COMMERCIAL INVENTION.

You know the story: Mother's Day wasn't started by some public-minded Oedipus. It was cooked up by a cabal of greeting card manufacturers, florists, and candy makers so they could sell more stuff. But are you going to resist this brazen manipulation? We thought not.

Start lobbying for National Tax Rebate Day.

MAY 15 ∽

YOU CANNOT HEEL YOUR INNER CHILD . . . OR MAKE IT SIT, ROLL OVER, PLAY DEAD, OR BEG.

The upside is, your inner child allows you to express yourself with gay abandon. The downside is that it does what it damn well pleases, and you have to spend a good part of each day trying to control the brat so it doesn't get you in trouble with your boss, your mate, your friends, or some menacing stranger on the street.

Look into obedience schools.

MAY 16 ∞

THE GOVERNMENT IN WASHINGTON IS THE REVENGE OF THE NERDS.

Think about who ran for student council in grade school: nerds. Kids who looked funny and who had names like Newt. And the same nerds keep running until they finally get into office. Then they start making nerd laws and policies.

Rebel. Tear all the warning tags off your pillows and mattresses.

MAY 17 ∞

BAMBI'S MOTHER WAS KILLED.

That's right. The hunter shot her. Not such a nice story after all, is it?

Support the right to arm bears.

MAY 18 ∽

BY TODAY'S STANDARDS, SOME OF YOUR BEST SEXUAL EXPERIENCES WOULD BE CONSIDERED DATE RAPE.

Remember that drunken night at the beach? The time the car ran out of gas? That passionate study-date at your dorm? Was permission asked for and explicitly given? Of course not; it was the moral equivalent of rape!

Send letters to your old lovers granting them retroactive permission.

MAY 19 ∞

YOUR MOTHER WILL ALWAYS BE ABLE TO PRESS A BUTTON THAT DRIVES YOU UP THE WALL.

No matter how grown-up you've become, how together you've gotten, how much you tell yourself you no longer care, your mother will still push your buttons.

Next time you go visit her or talk to her on the phone, put a piece of tin foil under your tongue. It won't help, but it will make you feel like you have some control over your pain.

MAY 20 ∞

YOU NEVER REALLY GOT RELIGION.

Countless people have found real comfort, support, and succor in religion. But not you. You're still sitting there waiting to get it. You know all the words, all the gestures, but you're faking the feelings.

Rent some football videotapes; look for ten Hail Mary passes.

MAY 21 ∾

BALD ISN'T SEXY.

Don't be fooled. The only reason a woman gets close to a bald-headed man is to use his chrome dome as a mirror so she can reapply her lipstick.

Call Sy Sperling—become a member.

MAY 22 ∾

THE SOCIAL SECURITY SYSTEM WILL RUN OUT BEFORE YOU HAVE A CHANCE TO COLLECT.

Ever since your first paycheck, you've been paying into a system that is supposed to give you your money back when you reach retirement age. And, as a matter of principle, you should get something back for your investment. Fat chance! Social Security used to be a sacred cow, but now the politicians have milked it dry.

Stay in shape—you may be working for a long time.

MAY 23 ∾

YOU WOULD BE BORED TO
TEARS BY A SIMPLE LIFE.

You'd be lost without your computer, microwave, mobile phone, and VCR. You're addicted to the conveniences of modern life.

Try going a week without watching TV; we dare you.

MAY 24 ∾

IF YOU GOT A NICE TAN LAST SUMMER,
YOU PROBABLY GOT A NICE
CASE OF SKIN CANCER, TOO.

It used to be that a tan was a sign of good health. Now it's the first stage of disease. Seems we've destroyed so much of the ozone layer that tanning is now the equivalent of suicide on the installment plan. So now we get to slather on sunblock, which hasn't been found to be carcinogenic—yet.

Buy lots of cool hats and sunglasses.

MAY 25 ∽

YOU ARE YOUR OWN CHEERLEADER
BECAUSE NO ONE ELSE CARES.

Give me an M, give me an E. What's that spell?
ME, ME, ME! You may as well look like an idiot and
do it; no one's going to watch. Make your inner child
join in.

Buy a pair of saddle shoes and a couple of pom-
poms.

MAY 26 ∽

EVERY YEAR YOU BECOME MORE
INTERESTED IN YOUR DIGESTION.

Remember when you were a kid and you couldn't figure out why adults talked about their digestion so much? Listen to a typical conversation with your friends: heartburn, gastritis, the runs, colitis, spastic colon, bulimia, high gorge, ulcers, and hemorrhoids. You think twice about that snack before bed now, don't you? And you know where to find the nicer bathrooms when you travel.

Go ahead, eat Mexican. Sure, you'll pay for it, but it'll give you something to talk about.

MAY 27 ∽

THE ONLY REFLECTION YOU'RE CAPABLE OF INVOLVES A MIRROR.

Look at yourself—no—not in the mirror. Look inside yourself. What do you see? Nothing? Need we say more?

Redecorate your living room with mirrored wall panels.

MAY 28 ∽

BATHING SUIT SEASON IS BACK.

It's time for the annual humiliation. How bad does your pasty flab look under those obnoxious fluorescent lights of a changing room?

Don't think about how many dollars an ounce they're asking for that bathing suit engineered out of dental floss.

MAY 29 ∞

NO ONE REMEMBERS WHAT
MEMORIAL DAY IS ABOUT,
AND NO ONE CARES.

These days, Memorial Day is just a good excuse for a sale, and the start of the summer rental season. But, when it started, it probably had something to do with the Revolutionary War, or maybe the Civil War, or perhaps Father Coughlin's Army of the Holocaust.

Find a parade and ask a veteran what it's all about. Shout so he can hear you.

MAY 30 ∞

YOUR STEPCHILDREN WISH
YOU WERE DEAD.

Large, happy, extended families only exist on TV. In reality, if you're a stepparent, you will always be seen as an usurper. You are unworthy of the family. A disgrace, an obstacle, an outsider. It's no accident that every stepparent in a fairy tale is evil: that's how kids feel.

Don't bother being nice to the brats, it won't help.

MAY 31 ∽

THERE WILL ALWAYS BE SOMEONE WHO KNOWS MORE THAN YOU DO.

Think you're pretty smart, don't you? Got all the answers? Know what's going on at all times? Well, we've got some bad news for you. There are people out there who've done more and know more. But, being the adaptable animal that you are, you search out people—consciously and unconsciously—who aren't as interesting, savvy, intelligent, or knowing as you. Why? So you can impart your own limited wisdom without feeling threatened or challenged. And the longer you stay away from those damn know-it-alls, the more fulfilling your life will seem.

Pick a topic to specialize in (e.g., Victorian bryophyte collectors).

JUNE 1 ∽

YOUR PARENTS LIED TO YOU.

That's right. Mr. and Mrs. Truth and Honesty were busy feeding you lines about the tooth fairy, Santa Claus, and the Easter Bunny. And you bought them all.

Rent *Nightmare on Elm Street* and root for Freddy.

JUNE 2 ∽

NO MATTER HOW GOOD A PARENT YOU ARE, YOUR CHILDREN WILL LIE TO YOU.

They have to, it's a part of their normal developmental-push-pull-antiestablishment-process thing. They're also very good at it. If you can afford one, hire a private investigator. Too pricey? Pay some of their friends to inform on them. Remember, when in doubt, they're lying.

Bug their rooms.

JUNE 3 ∞

YOU HAVE NO HEROES.

Your parents and grandparents had people they could look up to: heroes like Joe DiMaggio, Amelia Earhardt, and Mahatma Gandhi. But we've all become much too cynical for that. We know that sports stars are often compulsive gamblers, political leaders are owned by lobbyists, entertainers are drug addicts, and ministers have investigated sin a little more personally than necessary.

Dig up your old Superman and Batman comics.

JUNE 4 ∽

THE REALLY INTERESTING PEOPLE
SKIP SCHOOL REUNIONS.

Thinking about attending that class reunion so you can see the old gang? Don't bother. Reunions are basically a mass geek check designed to reveal those who don't have lives. Successful humans have other things to do. The only ones who attend are people who still haven't gotten over whatever good or bad things happened to them in school.

Drink a Fresca, read the old yearbook, and call a few classmates. It's the same experience as the reunion, without the travel expenses.

JUNE 5 ✍

CRAZY POSTAL WORKERS HANDLE
YOUR CORRESPONDENCE.

There are many different theories for why postal workers are so wacky. Maybe people soak their letters in LSD. Maybe it's the fact that the post office gives hiring preference to battle-shocked vets. Maybe it's the pressure of competing with Federal Express. But, face it, there seem to be more than a few loose nuts in the postal machine. This introduces a certain randomness to your bill payments, invitations, sweepstakes entries, and Dear John letters.

Go across town and mail yourself a letter. See how long it takes to arrive.

JUNE 6 ∞

STUDENTS GET AN ENTIRE
SUMMER OFF—YOU DON'T.

The weather's getting warm. Your attention span is getting shorter. And all those years of school have trained you to think that you can take July and August off and go on a surfin' safari. But you'll have to spend those lazy, hazy, crazy days of summer working your tail off at some job you hate.

Give a student a summer job and be a very strict boss.

JUNE 7 ∞

YOU'RE NOT HALF AS BRAVE
AS YOU THINK YOU ARE.

Sure, you'll talk a big game, but how brave are you really? When it comes to fight or flight, you're on the first supersonic transport out of there. And why not? You could get hurt, and with the ever-rising cost of health care, you'll have to take out a second mortgage for every hospital visit. Fighting's just not worth it. Pretty good rationalization, huh, wimp?

When you experience that next uncontrollable urge to do something brave, rent a video with Schwarzenegger in it until the feeling passes. No, not *Kindergarten Cop*—*The Terminator*.

JUNE 8 ∾

WHEN YOU'RE ALONE, YOU RELISH THE SMELL OF YOUR OWN FARTS.

You've had a second helping of Mom's old-fashioned Boston baked beans and your stomach is churning and boiling and reaching critical mass. Suddenly the pressure is too great, and something has to give. Instead of a burp, you fart. There's no noise, but the smell is undeniable. Luckily, you're not in a crowd of people but are alone in your bed. You inhale the noxious aroma and you smile. Sound familiar?

Include more fiber in your diet.

JUNE 9 ∽

CHEATERS PROSPER.

In a fair world, people who cheated would get caught and punished, and the good folks would reap the rewards. Unfortunately, that only happens in fairy tales. In the real world, cheaters get away with cheating all the time and make the honest plodders look like chumps.

Cut the cards; no sense in making it easier for cheaters than it is already.

JUNE 10 ∽

YOUR PARENTS WILL EMBARRASS YOU.

Getting ready to stand on your own two feet? Becoming your own person? Feeling independent? Relying on your parents less? Making friends on your own? Taking your parents for granted? Your friends are over and . . . Wham! Out come the stories about you when you were six years old and the time you went into the restaurant bathroom by yourself and decided to wash your hair with the soap. "You should have seen our little darling walking out of the men's room with a head full of lather. I think the waiters and waitresses are still laughing. And remember what you said? I'll never forget. You said, 'Look, Mommy, the shampoo here is great!'" This is the way your parents keep you in your place. They embarrass you in front of your friends as their way of reminding you that they come first, and don't you forget it.

Track down all your baby pictures and hide them in a safe place.

JUNE 11 ∽

A GOOD OFFENSE IS THE BEST DEFENSE.

The best way to get ahead in life is to never admit to anything. If, on those rare occasions, you find yourself having to defend an action or position, go on the offensive—be creative, and don't back down. For example, our editor felt this little dose of reality should have been deleted from the book. We quickly took the offensive and told her it might be a good idea that she take this matter up with her therapist, because obviously she's dealing with unresolved Oedipal attachment issues coupled with poor object-relations in the rapprochement subphase of development.

Pick up a secondhand Psychology 101 textbook.

JUNE 12 ∾

YOU'D BE LOST IN THE WOODS.

Quick: Which way is north? Don't have a clue, do you? You might survive in the urban jungle, but how would you fare in the peaceful, sylvan woods that are home to such adorable creatures as Bambi, Peter Rabbit, and Smokey the Bear? Take away your satellite-activated directional finder, your cellular phone, your butane lighter, your Big Mac and fries, your semiautomatic assault rifle, and you're dead meat.

Don't tempt fate. If you must see rocks and trees, go to a museum.

JUNE 13 ∽

MICROWAVES, CELLULAR PHONES, CD PLAYERS, CABLE TV, AND CAMCORDERS WITH LARGER-THAN-LIFE VIEWFINDERS CAUSE CANCER.

Chances are you own at least one of these, but take heart—you're not alone. Misery loves company. Besides, those people who eschew modern electronics are either hermits, misanthropes, psychopaths, or Amish.

Go out with a bang. Record yourself heating up a chili dog in the microwave; turn on HBO, crank up the CD player, and call a friend from your cellular phone.

JUNE 14 ∽

DOGS EAT SHIT.

Ever wonder why a puppy's breath is so bad when he licks you? Just take a look at what he eats when he is wandering loose in the yard. You shouldn't be surprised: look at how dogs greet each other.

Think twice about letting a dog lick your face.

JUNE 15 ∽

YOU PAY A LARGER PERCENTAGE OF YOUR INCOME IN TAXES THAN THE REALLY RICH DO.

If you didn't pay your fair share of taxes, you'd get fined and go to jail. But there are multimillionaires in this country who pay little or nothing, and they do it legally. The system is set up so that once you are really rich, it's in your interest to hire accountants and lawyers who can find existing loopholes for you or support politicians who will put special loopholes into the tax code just for you. It's legal. It sucks. It's a fact.

Pay your taxes. If you can't be superrich, at least you can feel morally superior to those who are.

JUNE 16 ∽

YOU ARE ONE CRITICISM AWAY FROM
A NERVOUS BREAKDOWN.

Your self-esteem is so low that if someone so much as criticizes your choice of music, your clothes, or your haircut, you go into an emotional tailspin.

Buy some ear plugs.

JUNE 17 ∽

THE ONLY REASON YOU AREN'T
EVEN MORE CODEPENDENT IS
BECAUSE MOST PEOPLE AVOID YOU.

You may be pretty independent, but ask yourself this: Am I independent because I want to be, or because I have to be? If the really neat clique in high school had asked you to join, you would have.

Learn all the words to the Barney song.

JUNE 18 ∾

CRYING DURING MOVIES IS WIMPY.

You believe your date thinks you're sensitive if you let yourself go and cry during some sappy scene in a movie. Well, you're wrong. What you're doing is exposing a weakness that will be used against you later.

Do research before going to the movies. If you think there's a chance you might turn on the emotional waterworks, build an alibi; tell your date you're coming down with a cold.

JUNE 19 ∽

IF YOU DIE, THE PEOPLE WHO GET YOUR CHILDREN WILL MISTREAT THEM.

You connect with your children on thousands of levels. You can tell their cries from those of other babies, and you can tell by the cry how serious the problem is. You can read their faces, and their body language, and you know when you need to spend some quality time together. No one else can do this. To them, the hurt silences are stubbornness, and the clingy, needy episodes are signs of weakness. So, if you go, your kids are in for a real shock.

Make as much money as you can; people will treat the kids better if they're rich.

JUNE 20 ∾

CHILDBIRTH HURTS.

Of course, we don't know this from personal experience, but we've heard things—scary things. Like how can a little baby's head possibly fit through an opening that small? Ouch! It hurts just thinking about it.

Pop *The Exorcist* into the VCR and play Linda Blair's possession scenes in very slow motion.

JUNE 21 ∽

AIRLINES ARE CUTTING BACK ON MAINTENANCE.

When commercial airlines started, they did everything they could to inspire confidence: captains were the brightest, engineers were the best. Everyone was proud to be in the aviation business, and they kept their planes in perfect shape. Now airlines are a down-and-dirty business. Sullen employees who are mad at management give the aircraft the same careful attention they give your luggage.

Keep flying. The trains are worse, and buses are unspeakably bad.

JUNE 22 ∾

IF YOU DON'T TAKE CHARGE OF YOUR LIFE, SOMEONE ELSE WILL.

Think you can just sit there and watch the world go by? Well, think again. There are lots of people who would be happy to point you in a direction that works for them. They'll make you the workhorse of the family or the whipping boy of their company.

Get assertive. Drive in the passing lane.

JUNE 23 ∾

WHEN KIDS SAY SOMETHING'S BAD, YOU AREN'T SURE WHAT THEY MEAN.

It's difficult enough that *gay* doesn't mean *happy* anymore, and *straight* doesn't mean *honest*, but now *bad* can mean *bad*, or it can mean *good*. So, if a kid says a CD is *bad*, does he want it or not?

Limit conversations with kids to questions that can be answered yes or no, or, more likely, uh-huh or nah.

123

JUNE 24 ∞

HOW DO YOU KNOW YOU
CAN'T TAKE IT WITH YOU?

You know someone who's come back from the dead or something? We don't think so. We also think there's some heavy lobbying being done by the survivors-of-dead-people group. They've got us believing that before you leave this earth, you must donate all the stuff you've accumulated or give it to family and friends. What a bunch of garbage. Let them get their own stuff.

Buy an extra coffin.

JUNE 25 ∽

WORRYING ABOUT HYPERTENSION
CAUSES HYPERTENSION.

Doctors say high blood pressure is worth worrying about—but don't worry too much, because that will cause high blood pressure. There's no easy way to know if you have it: doctors say you have to go to doctors to find out.

Take up yoga.

JUNE 26 ∽

YOU LIE THROUGH YOUR TEETH.

You think you're telling people what they want to hear in order to placate them, when, in actuality, you're deceiving them. You have your own agenda and you'll do what it takes to get what you want. That's a fact of life and we're not lying—this time.

Spend a second or two feeling guilty, then get on with your life.

JUNE 27 ∽

YOU'RE NOT THAT UNDERSTANDING, IT'S YOUR CODEPENDENT NEED TO BE LIKED.

Friends are so important to you, you'll do whatever it takes to keep them. You'll also tell them whatever they want to hear because you can't stand the idea that a friend might stop liking you. Pretty pathetic, huh? Not that you're pathetic. Not at all. In fact, you're just fine. We understand where you're coming from.

Please be our friend.

JUNE 28 ∞

TIME DRAGS WHEN YOU HATE
WHAT YOU'RE DOING.

We all know that time flies when you're having fun; but what about the 97 percent of the time when you're not having fun? Does it fly when you're at work? When you're filling out insurance forms? When you're waiting for your number to come up at the deli counter? When you're waiting for the dryer to finish?

Daydream.

JUNE 29 ∞

YOU HAVE TO DIE TO GO TO HEAVEN.

Heaven—the everlasting reward. Sounds great, but think what you have to go through to get there. Your body has to stop cold. Everything clogs up. You're paralyzed, you lose control of your bowels, you're fertilizer.

Go toward the light . . . now turn it off; you're wasting electricity.

JUNE 30 ∞

YOUR CONCEPTION WAS A LAST-DITCH EFFORT TO KEEP YOUR PARENTS' MARRIAGE TOGETHER.

You were the glue that was supposed to bond your parents back together. If they could focus their energies on you, they wouldn't have to deal with each other. What a plan. And what do you do? You dash their hopes by demanding your independence. You go off to school, move out, or worse, get married. How selfish, especially after everything they did to keep the family together. You should be ashamed of yourself.

Move back home *immediately*.

JULY 1 ⚬

PRISONS ARE OVERCROWDED, SO
THEY'RE SETTING CRIMINALS FREE.

It used to be that prison was prison, and you had to be really, really good to get a "Get Out of Jail" card. Now you just have to be less evidently evil than some more recently nabbed felon.

Check references.

JULY 2 ∞

THIS YEAR IS HALF OVER, AND
YOU'VE DONE NOTHING

Where does the time go? It feels like it was just yesterday when you—once again—made all those great and wonderful New Year's resolutions. Well, now it's six months later, and what have you accomplished? You're still overweight; you haven't asked for that raise; and you have yet to crack open that 365-days-to-a-better-vocabulary book you bought yourself. When was the last time you accomplished just one of those many masochistic resolutions you made?

Throw a midyear New Year's Eve party. Make some new resolutions, but keep them simple, like promise to buy yourself some new socks and underwear or vow to give up brussels sprouts.

JULY 3 ∞

FISH SHIT IN WATER.

Every health and diet book you read tells you to drink gallons of water. But remember the time you looked at a drop of pond water under a microscope in school? The water was full of squiggly things. And think of the last stream you saw: if it wasn't full of old tires and rusting shopping carts, it was teeming with frogs and fish who were busy pumping out eggs, milt, and feces.

Order a double espresso: any creatures in it will be boiled to death, and you'll never taste the other stuff through the coffee.

JULY 4 ∽

PATRIOTISM IS DEAD.

Think this holiday is about patriotism? No way. The holiday is about getting rowdy and overeating. Every year, dozens of fingers are lost to firecrackers, hundreds of dogs have nervous breakdowns, and thousands of people are poisoned by spoiled mayonnaise.

Go for the hot dogs; the egg salad could kill you.

JULY 5 ∽

ALL THE GOOD REAL ESTATE
DEALS ARE GONE.

If real estate was a game of musical chairs, you'd be one of the chumps who get left standing. All the property with views: gone. All the property on the shore: taken. All the undervalued property: snapped up by sharks looking for big profits.

Buy a Winnebago.

JULY 6 ∽

YOU'RE IN A DEAD-END JOB.

You already know this. The last thing you want is to be reminded again. In fact, everything was going just fine until we had to bring up this issue. What the hell were we thinking? One of the reasons you're reading this book is so you can get your mind off your nowhere job. We messed up. Can you accept our apologies?

Accept our apologies.

JULY 7 ∽

YOUR BODY IS COVERED WITH MICROSCOPIC PARASITES.

You've got bacteria swarming on your skin, mites camping out in your eyelids, and all manner of tiny parasitic things festering in your intestines—and so does that really tasty someone you've been thinking about cuddling with.

Ask your accountant if you can claim those parasites as dependents.

JULY 8 ∽

IF YOU DIE SUDDENLY,
THE WORLD WILL NOT END.

Sorry, but that's the truth. Sure, you'll be missed for a while, but time does wonders for one's memory. And think of the benefits your family and friends will derive from your passing. Your loved one will have the whole bed to him or herself, a coworker will have one less person to compete against, and a friend will finally get his or her hands on your collection of bootleg Beatles tapes.

Write to the Hemlock Society for all their free pamphlets and brochures.

JULY 9 ∽

THERE ARE OVER 2 BILLION
OTHER PEOPLE ON THE PLANET.

You are just one of many, many, many, many, many people. Few of your actions have any more consequence than a pebble dropped into the Pacific.

Have a nice day.

JULY 10 ∽

IF YOU'RE READING THIS BOOK
PAGE BY PAGE, YOU HAVE
TOO MUCH FREE TIME.

Or your TV's busted. Or you're killing time at the local bookstore. In fact, you're probably in one of those new book stores with a damned coffee bar and you're sipping a wimpy decaf capuccino and getting decaf latte stains all over the cover. And you're chuckling to yourself and dog-earing all the pages that you think are amusing, and . . . Hey, we get it, you have no intention of paying for this book. You're a thief. Either buy the book or put it back on the shelf where you got it right now. What did you say!? Take that back or else . . . That's it, we're calling the cops.

Call the cops. Turn yourself in.

JULY 11 ∽

EVEN IF YOU DO SOMETHING PERFECTLY,
SOMEONE ELSE WILL REVISE IT.

The world is full of amateur editors who look at your work the way a dog looks at a hydrant. It doesn't matter how right something is, they won't be happy until they've made their mark on it.

Smile sweetly, then ignore the changes.

JULY 12 ∽

DO YOU KNOW WHERE YOUR
TV REMOTE IS?

How many hours have you lost looking for the remote to your TV—hours you could have spent writing the great American novel, taming your inner child, or furthering your career? It's a question of priorities, and we know what yours are.

Invest in a pager and strap it to your remote. Whenever you misplace that pesky piece of plastic, dial the pager from your phone and voilà, the beeper tells you where it is. *Note:* Make sure the beeper is switched to audible; the vibrating mode ain't going to do squat.

JULY 13 ∽

VIRGINS DON'T KNOW WHAT THEY'RE DOING.

Even before they became the safest kind of sex partner (but, of course, not completely safe—it is theoretically possible for there to be a junkie virgin), people always raved about the glory of deflowering virgins. But what's the point? At best, virgins are scared and clumsy. At worst, they may cry for days.

Stick to people with the same kind of mileage on them that you've got; leave the virgins to each other.

JULY 14 ∾

ON AVERAGE, IT TAKES FOUR TIMES
MORE TIME TO PREPARE A
MEAL THAN TO EAT ONE.

Cut, chop, boil, simmer, bake, sauté, braise, roast, puree, whip, frappé, pound, blacken, grill, carve, smoke, and broil. What happened to TV dinners and Minute rice? If we only had to take some pill for our daily nutrition, we'd have more time to solve the problems of the world.

Look up *frappé* and call us with the definition.

JULY 15 ∞

THE AIRBAGS IN CARS HAVE
NEVER BEEN TESTED.

Air bags use a system with motion detectors hooked to tiny switches that trigger chemicals that create gas that inflates bags that pop out of containers in microseconds. Does this sound like a system that will break, or what? Companies can't even make condoms with a 100 percent quality record. How well do you think they'll do with a system that sounds like it was designed by Rube Goldberg?

Ask for an air bag demo next time you shop for cars.

JULY 16 ∽

YOU CAN'T PROTECT YOUR CHILDREN.

So you think you're the great protector. You buy the best cornstarch on the market because you don't want your child to suffer from diaper rash. You look both ways before you cross the street with the stroller. You make sure the cables are secure before you take little junior in the elevator. You think you have everything covered, don't you? Have you stopped to consider that some night when you're sleeping soundly in your bed a band of babynapping ninja warriors could steal into your kid's room and whisk him or her off before you can say banzai? How about an earthquake? A two-seater Cessna that loses power in one of its engines and smashes into the side of your house? Maybe mole men from the center of the earth who come to the surface in search of a new Mole King or Queen and discover that your child would be perfect? Need we say more?

Teach your children how to dial 911.

JULY 17 ∽

WHEN YOU CALL IN SICK,
NO ONE BELIEVES YOU.

Somewhere along the line, you'll get sick. And no matter how dedicated you are, when you call to tell your coworkers or boss that you just can't make it in to work, you'll hear a hint of disbelief in the voice on the other end of the line.

Get a note from your doctor.

JULY 18 ∽

YOU CAN'T REMEMBER THE WORDS
TO THE NATIONAL ANTHEM.

Go ahead, try. It starts with the name *José* and the last two words are *play ball*. You probably can't remember the words to the "Pledge of Allegiance," either. (Hint: "I fed the pigeons to the flag.") Either you're a traitor at heart, or your memory's going.

Sew a flag patch onto your windbreaker so everyone will know you're true blue.

JULY 19 ∾

TO BIRDS, YOU ARE A TARGET.

No matter how natty you are when you leave the house, there's always a chance that some bird will put a deposit down on your jacket or add some doo to your hairdo.

Try for revenge: use the bathroom every time you fly.

JULY 20 ∽

YOU STILL DON'T KNOW HOW
TO PROGRAM YOUR VCR.

How long have you had that thing? You've spent good money on a machine that can record your favorite shows and you don't have a clue how to program it. All you know how to do is play the movies you rent at your local video store. How pathetic. You have the technology, yet all you can do is piss and moan when your boss says you have to stay late at work because you're going to miss *NYPD Blue*, *Northern Exposure*, or repeats of *Cheers*.

Find some ten-year-old in the neighborhood and give him a couple of bucks to show you how your VCR works.

JULY 21 ∞

IF YOUR CLOTHES LOOK GOOD TO YOUR FRIENDS, THEY'LL LOOK HORRIBLE TO YOUR PARENTS, AND VICE VERSA.

Everyone has an idea of just how they want you to look. When you dress to impress your friends, your parents are mortified. What if one of their friends saw you looking that way? But if you bump into the gang on the one day when you begrudgingly don the togs Mom and Dad gave you for your birthday, they'll quickly point out how dorky you look.

Dress for your friends. Your parents are stuck with you.

JULY 22 ∽

NO MATTER WHAT YOU DO, IT'S NOT GOING TO BE YOUR WEDDING.

Weddings are for the parents of the bride, since they're the ones who are usually footing the bill. Sure, it's your day, but watch how quickly that changes when you two want a rock 'n' roll band and her parents want Scottish bagpipers.

Try on those tartans and start taking Highland fling lessons.

JULY 23 ∽

WORK ISN'T MEANT TO BE FUN.

It's called work because it's not fun. If it were fun, they wouldn't pay you to do it.

Be sure to use all your sick days.

JULY 24 ∽

FORTY-NINE PERCENT OF ALL DOCTORS WERE IN THE BOTTOM HALF OF THEIR MEDICAL SCHOOL CLASS.

Scary thought, huh? Even if your doctor went to a prestigious medical school, how do you know he or she didn't mess up big time and just squeak by? You never know. Maybe that white-coated, stethoscope-draped miracle worker still can't tell the difference between simple indigestion and an advanced ulcer.

Write to the AMA and tell them to force the medical schools to list doctors' ranking on their diplomas and provide each patient with a detailed transcript.

JULY 25 ∾

THE SELF-HELP MOVEMENT ENCOURAGES PEOPLE TO BE SELFISH.

It used to be when people got religion, they became generous and did volunteer work. Now, when they get fanatical, they focus on themselves. The only thing that matters is their own trauma and the fact that they got a bike instead of a pony at age eight is as big a tragedy as a fire that destroys an orphanage.

Practice saying "Get over it."

JULY 26 ∽

MAYBE YOUR HIGHER POWER
DOESN'T LIKE YOU.

Your Higher Power can only be so tolerant. How many times do you think it can put up with you getting so drunk you throw up all over yourself? Or watching you stay in a relationship with some person who's obviously cheating on you? Or coping with your decision to remain in a dead-end job with no chance of advancement?

Buy your Higher Power some flowers and make reservations at a fancy restaurant.

JULY 27 ∽

GETTING STONED DOESN'T MAKE YOU MORE CREATIVE, JUST LESS DISCRIMINATING.

When you're stoned, you can spend hours contemplating the fascinating patterns in the hairs on your arm. Not the most creative of pastimes. Try and explain a joke you laughed at when you were stoned and you'll find it doesn't make sense. And forget about reading anything you wrote while baked.

Fess up. Creativity has nothing to do with it. You like getting stupid.

JULY 28 ∽

YOU ARE NOT AS SUPPORTIVE
A FRIEND AS YOU THINK.

How much would you really do for a friend?
Would you lend him or her money? And if so, how
much? Five dollars? Fifty dollars? Five hundred dollars? And what if he forgot to pay you back? Would
you remind him? Send an anonymous note? Have another friend mention it? Or would you just let it go
and eventually resent him? Your call. Enjoy.

Quick, borrow money from your friends before
they borrow some from you.

JULY 29 ∾

YOUR PET DOESN'T
UNDERSTAND ENGLISH.

You talk to your dog: praise it, scold it, and confide in it. But all the mutt hears is tone of voice. You could speak in Urdu, pig Latin, or use names from the phone book or the Congressional Record and get the same results.

Use whatever foreign language you learned in school. It'll impress the neighbors.

JULY 30 ∾

YOU ARE A TAKER.

"Buy me, give me, take me." Sound familiar? It should. It's what your inner child really wants. Deep down inside, you're spoiled. You have to be, because if you don't take everything you can, someone else will. You're only doing what every other person in this world is doing; you're protecting your self-interest. If you don't, who's going to? You've got to fight for what's yours. Go get 'em, tiger.

Make a cake and eat it.

JULY 31 ∾

WHEN SOMEONE SAYS, "LET ME SHARE THIS WITH YOU," THEY ARE ABOUT TO ATTACK.

For years, assertiveness training, EST, and advanced life insurance sales classes all taught the same manipulative technique: When you want to shove one of your opinions down someone's throat, start by saying, "Let me share this with you." So if a person utters this phrase when they're not holding a piece of pie and two forks, it's time to get your guard up.

Learn to use the word *no*.

AUGUST 1 ∾

THERE IS NO SUCH THING AS A FREE LUNCH.

O.K., so this isn't the most original comment. But it's one that's worth remembering, nonetheless. Free lunch means the bozo picking up the tab will talk your ear off and then call in a month and remind you that you owe him a favor.

Brown bag it.

AUGUST 2 ∞

A MILLION PEOPLE ARE WALKING
AROUND ON PROZAC.

People are popping antidepressants and other mood-soothing drugs like candy. The country is starting to look like a 1950s zombie movie or a scene out of *The Stepford Wives*. Agitated that at some future date you or your dog might suffer from the heartbreak of psoriasis? Take some Zoloft. Having trouble controlling your hair color? Try some Paxil. Favorite sitcom in reruns? Pop some Anafranil.

Get the woozy pill heads to play high-stakes poker with you.

AUGUST 3 ∞

YOU'VE FINALLY FOUND YOURSELF!
BIG DEAL.

Do you really think anyone cares that you've found inner peace, nirvana, enlightenment, or whatever they call it nowadays? As a matter of fact, most people would be jealous. How dare you walk around with that beatific, I've-seen-it-all, there's-something-better-than-material-goods-and-steamy-sex look on your face, while the rest of us are trying to make ends meet and keep up our car payments. You make us sick with that holier-than-thou, I'm-better-than-you attitude. Keep those damn feelings to yourself. Remember what happened to Jesus Christ.

Practice lashing a couple of sticks together in the form of a cross—just in case.

AUGUST 4 ∾

OUR MILITARY'S FIRST OBJECTIVE IS TO PRESERVE THE MILITARY—NOT TO PROTECT YOU.

To the military, all civilians are suspect. You might be a collaborator. Or worse, someone who thinks that feeding children is more important than designing really expensive jets that can fly without crashing—almost. They'd shoot you in a heartbeat if it would get them money for another missile.

Become an international arms dealer.

AUGUST 5 ∞

IN A CRISIS SITUATION, YOU FALL APART.

You've run the scenarios through your head a million times. You're in a bar and a drunk starts to bother you. Wham! He's out like a light. Terrorists have taken the World Trade Center hostage. Zap! They're history. The pilot has a heart attack just before landing. Zing! No problem. Who the heck are you kidding? Come on back to the real world. How many times have you fallen to pieces because there's no milk for your morning coffee? How many puddles of sweat have you left in various reception areas while waiting for that important interview to happen? How many boxes of tissues have you gone through once you discovered they were preempting *NYPD Blue*?

Stock up on paper products.

AUGUST 6 ∽

YOU'RE DOOMED TO SPENDING COUNTLESS HOURS TALKING TO MACHINES.

Technology has won. Practically every phone call is completed now due to the proliferation of the ubiquitous (and often annoying) answering machine (*see March 22—Your Answering Machine Message Stinks*) or the call is stuck in some phone mail hell.

Pretend you have a rotary phone and insist on talking to a human voice.

AUGUST 7 ∽

IF YOU WANT TO BE LOVED, YOU'D BETTER BE WILLING TO PAY FOR IT.

Love does not come cheap. Think of those flowers, chocolates, and cards as an investment. Because with love, like everything else, you get what you pay for.

Buy stock in Hallmark.

AUGUST 8 ∽

YOUR DRIVE WILL GO DOWN AND YOUR DISKS WILL GIVE YOU TROUBLE.

Computer technology has made us much more efficient and much more dependent. Disk drives don't freeze up often; only when you really need them. And disks will only fail when there's something crucial on them.

Back up, or go manual.

AUGUST 9 ∽

YOUR DISKS WILL GIVE YOU TROUBLE AND YOUR DRIVE WILL GO DOWN.

If you sit, walk, or lie down in the course of your average day, sooner or later your back will act up. The disks will deform, a nerve will get pinched, and you'll discover a whole new realm of pain that will affect every part of your body. In response, you'll get cautious and shy away from all sorts of challenges and opportunities.

Back down, or go digital.

AUGUST 10 ∽

BE AFRAID, BE VERY AFRAID.

Did you know that you could have an aneurysm in your brain and it could explode at any second? Did you know that Iraq has enough plutonium to make a hydrogen bomb? Did you realize how easy it is to contaminate the water in our reservoirs? Did you ever think that there's a 50 percent chance that your significant other will leave you for someone else? Did you stop to consider that while you're reading this, one of your coworkers is trying to get you fired?

Don't worry, be happy.

AUGUST 11 ∽

BARTENDERS, HAIRDRESSERS, AND PERSONAL TRAINERS DON'T REALLY CARE WHAT YOU THINK.

They may nod politely, smile, and seem to hang on your every word, but the only reason they do that is to put you in a generous tipping mood. You are their customer, not their friend.

Don't tell them anything you wouldn't be willing to see in the tabloids.

AUGUST 12 ∞

YOU HAVE NO IDEA WHERE
YOUR TAX DOLLARS GO.

You spend a good part of every year working to support Uncle Sam, but do you have any idea what Sammy does with your dollars? Not really. Ask a politician about the black budget—the budget that pays for all the Stealth bombers that didn't crash because they didn't yet exist. All he'll tell you is that it doesn't go into his pockets. But somehow almost every president and congressperson retires a lot richer than when they started.

Send for some free government booklets; it gives you a sense that you're getting something back.

AUGUST 13 ∞

ONLY THE STRONG SURVIVE.

Darwin was right when he came up with his "survival of the fittest" theory.

Save up your money. The strong may be fierce, but they can be bought, too.

AUGUST 14 ∽

ANY REALLY GOOD TIME WILL BE
FOLLOWED BY A HANGOVER.

It's as if the human body was set up to say, "I told you so." Have a few drinks, get a headache. Play too hard, wake up sore. If you really let loose, you pay.

Take the aspirin and water before you collapse. Start your recovery in your sleep.

AUGUST 15 ∽

YOU HAVE A BORING ROLE
IN THE PLAY OF LIFE.

"All the world's a stage," and you're still waiting in the wings. When are you going to understand that this is not a dress rehearsal? Slap on the grease paint, enter the clowns, hoist that spear with dignity. The chorus awaits. All you need to do is remember your lines. You do remember your lines, don't you?

Plays suck, anyway. Wait for your life to come out on cable.

AUGUST 16 ∞

YOUR DREAMS ARE MEANINGLESS.

Charlatans of all stripes will claim to be able to interpret your dreams. They will reveal deep symbolisms and important revelations. The problem is, our dreams are basically pretty random, and about as meaningful as tea leaves or the bumps on your skull.

Roll over and go back to sleep.

AUGUST 17 ∞

YOU HAVE A NEGATIVE ATTITUDE.

You're always putting everyone down. You don't have a nice thing to say about anything or anybody. And your negative attitude will keep you from succeeding or ever being happy.

Start by repeating, "I think I can, I think I can, I think I can . . ."

AUGUST 18 ∽

YOU'RE A CLOSET BIGOT.

Deep in your heart, you really believe that other kinds of people are inferior. You're even afraid of some of them, and no, you don't want them marrying your sister. But unlike Archie Bunker, you're not honest enough to admit it.

Move to Montana.

AUGUST 19 ∽

YOUR BODY IS SHRINKING.

It happens when you age. The cumulative effects of gravity take an inch or two off your height. Pretty soon you'll be hiking your waistband up to your armpits so you won't trip on your cuffs. Can't afford to trip with brittle bones, you know.

Start using a cane now when it's still a fashion accessory, not a necessity.

AUGUST 20 ∾

YOU REALLY DO SOUND LIKE THE
VOICE ON THE TAPE RECORDER.

You know how reedy and thin your voice sounds on a tape recorder? That's what you sound like to everybody but yourself. That sexier, more resonant sound is merely the effect of hearing your voice through your own thick skull.

Listen to yourself on tape. Think about the sound. You know that voice. (*See January 11—You Are Becoming More and More Like Your Parents.*)

AUGUST 21 ⤨

MOST TEN-YEAR-OLDS ARE BETTER
WITH COMPUTERS THAN YOU ARE.

How many times have you had to wait for your preteen child or some neighbor's kid to come home from a play date or finish watching reruns of *The Jetsons* because you couldn't remember how to access the software you needed to finish that big proposal that was due the next morning? Pretty humiliating, huh? Not only are these kids better with computers, they're better with most of today's consumer electronics (*see July 20—You Still Don't Know How to Program Your VCR*).

After the brat gets you online, brag about how much later you can stay up on school nights.

AUGUST 22 ∾

IF YOUR COMPUTER DIDN'T HAVE SPELL CHECK, YOU'D PROBABLY LOSE YOUR JOB.

It's sickening how dependent we are on computers. Our lives revolve around what's in our computer's memory. Have you backed up your files? How do you know your computer doesn't have a virus? It could be eating all your files right this second. Pretty scary, huh?

Take two aspirins and call the computer doctor in the morning.

AUGUST 23 ∾

YOU WATCH TOO MUCH TELEVISION.

You're probably watching the old boob tube right now, and if you're not, it's because the set's either broken or you're at work and your boss won't let you. As soon as you get home tonight, you'll grab the remote and turn on the idiot box even before you put the keys down. You hate the quiet and you're lonely—oh, so lonely. The silence is deafening. You can't stand it. You break out into a cold sweat and your teeth start chattering. You lunge for the remote control, shakily aim it at the TV, and hit the on button. You're pathetic.

We misplaced the local TV listings. Would you give us a call and tell us what's on cable tonight?

AUGUST 24 ❧

YOUR HIGHER POWER MAY BE HIGH.

Fine, you've accepted the existence of some Higher Power; but what's to say that Higher Power isn't busy getting high? That's what Higher Powers do. When you have some free time, do you worry about what you can do to make mosquitoes and microbes happy? No, you get off on caffeine, alcohol, TV, religion, or some other narcotic.

Imitate your Higher Power, however you conceive her.

AUGUST 25 ∽

EVERY SECOND THAT PASSES MEANS
YOU'RE CLOSER TO DEATH.

Hate being reminded that you're mortal, huh? Remember those teen years? Nothing could stop you. You were Superman; you could leap any building, race a bullet, and you were more powerful than a locomotive. Now look at you. Not only are you closer to death, but you're deteriorating right before your own eyes. By the way, isn't it about time you had your prescription checked?

Go to the doctor. Memorize the eye chart first.

AUGUST 26 ∞

TRANSFUSIONS COULD KILL YOU.

You've been severely injured, and your blood gauge is creeping toward E. They find you in time and start to fill you up again. Odds are you'll go on to a nice long life. But just maybe they bought the blood from some addict who needed the money for his next fix. They screen out most of those folks, but some slip through.

Carry a spare pint of blood with you at all times.

AUGUST 27 ∞

YOU ARE RESPONSIBLE FOR YOUR OWN ACTIONS.

Don't try to blame your parents. And it's not the fault of society, the economy, or the people who were bad influences in your life. Don't even think of trying to blame your actions on your inner child or on a Higher Power. It's you and only you.

Forget it if you think we're going to give you an action on this one.

AUGUST 28 ∽

DOCTORS DON'T UNDERSTAND CANCER.

When cancer strikes, doctors get full of maybes, probablys, and we thinks. Ask a doctor if they killed the cancer they operated, radiated, and chemoed and your doctor will say, "If it doesn't recur in five years, we will determine that we got it." It's pretty clear that they're faking it and playing for time.

Tell the doctor you maybe, probably, think you can pay him someday.

AUGUST 29 ∽

YOU'VE NEVER EXPERIENCED A
FULL-BODY ORGASM.

Sure, you've experienced the simple orgasm where your eyes roll in the back of your head and your breathing becomes short and labored. You may even have done that shuddering, quivering thing. But have you ever felt that sensation where your whole body goes into an ecstatic, massive electric shock state? We doubt it.

Make sure your medical insurance is paid up, just in case.

AUGUST 30 ∽

YOU HAVE NO IDEA WHETHER YOUR
THERAPIST IS COMPETENT.

He or she may be brilliant, but he or she may also be a sick, perverted psychopath who loves to hear other people's problems. Consider the silences: Is it the therapist's suppressed rage? Hostility? Maybe late onset autism?

Try to make the dummy talk. You're paying for the session, aren't you? (Hint: Tell the therapist you're deducting $10 from the payment for each time you hear "Hmmmm" or "How did that make you feel?")

AUGUST 31 ∽

YOU LOOK SILLY IN A WOOLEN CAP.

The only people who should wear woolen caps are convicts, mental patients, and sailors. Not only does a woolen cap make the wearer look like someone out of an institution, but it gives a terminal case of hat head (*see April 13—There Is No Cure for Hat Head*). Take it from us, if you wear a woolen cap, no one will ever take you seriously again.

Throw out those "cute" little woolen mittens, too.

SEPTEMBER 1 ∽

YOUR EYES ARE GOING.

Type of this size is legal for most documents. The assumption is that the majority of the population will have no trouble reading it. But it looks pretty small, doesn't it? As people age, their sight goes . . . their joints ache . . . their back gets stiff . . . their hair falls out . . .

Stop eating carrots. It's too late.

SEPTEMBER 2 ∾

YOU ONLY READ THE HEADLINES.

You're as deep as twenty-four-point type. The smaller print of the article doesn't interest you one whit. All you want is enough information so you can sound like you know what you're talking about.... Wait a minute. What are we doing? You're not even reading this. Why are we wasting our time?

Pick up a copy of the *New York Times* large-print edition. Maybe you'll learn something.

SEPTEMBER 3 ∾

IF A SONG IS GOOD, IT WILL BE PLAYED TO DEATH AND THEN RUINED IN A TV COMMERCIAL.

Every now and then a song comes along that reaches you, that moves your soul. Until you've heard it for the 1,200th time. Then it gets a little old. And by the time you've heard some bogus version in the background of a light beer or feminine hygiene product commercial for the 4,000th time, you've learned to hate it.

Don't hum it—it'll stay in your head all day long!

SEPTEMBER 4 ∽

THE LABOR MOVEMENT IS DEAD.

In its day, the labor movement was full of ideas and relevance; now all that's left are some songs hippies know and some jokes. Here's one: How many teamsters does it take to screw in a light bulb? Twelve! You got a problem with that, buddy? Maybe you'd like a strike! Here's the chant: "What do we want? More ties with organized crime! When do we want it? On one of the four days of the year that aren't union holidays!"

Celebrate Labor Day in the most appropriate way: take the day off.

SEPTEMBER 5 ∾

WHEN YOU SURVIVE, YOU'RE
SUBJECT TO SURVIVOR'S GUILT.

When bad things happen, if you're strong or lucky, you'll survive. But you won't get to feel good about it. You may have dodged a big bullet, but others didn't, so just when you should feel victorious, you're bummed out.

Go on the lecture circuit and talk about your survival. Dedicate your comments to those who didn't make it (but keep the fees).

SEPTEMBER 6 ∽

FACE IT, YOU CAN'T UNDERSTAND
HOW THE KIDS OF TODAY
CAN LISTEN TO THAT NOISE.

This one hits a lot of buttons. Who would have thought it? Hendrix, Morrison, and Joplin, the lionized pantheon of a day gone by, are considered classics today, or even worse, elevator music, while Nine Inch Nails, Stone Temple Pilots, and Green Day are this generation's junk du jour.

Write your congressperson, tell him or her you want a special day commemorating Iron Butterfly and that "In-A-Gadda-Da-Vida" should be the new national anthem.

SEPTEMBER 7 ∽

YOU'RE A WHORE.

You'd do almost anything for a million bucks, right? That makes you a whore. A high-priced whore, but a whore, nonetheless.

Raise your rates.

SEPTEMBER 8 ∽

IF YOU FEEL BAD WHEN YOU'RE SICK, IMAGINE HOW THOSE WHO HAVE TO TAKE CARE OF YOU FEEL.

"I'm zic. Could you had me a dissue? I'm ready for my chicken zoup now. Is it time for me to take my medicine? Would you pwump my pilwow? I don't feel good, make me better." How long would your patience last if you had to deal with a patient like this?

Contact Dr. Kervorkian.

SEPTEMBER 9 ∽

YOU WILL ALWAYS BE A CHILD TO YOUR PARENTS.

Even if you were elected president, won a Nobel prize, walked on the moon, and raised your own family, you'll still be just a kid to your parents. They'll still consider you unformed, and they'll still try and give you advice.

Ask your parents to raise your allowance.

SEPTEMBER 10 ∽

SELF-DISCOVERY IS DEPRESSING AND TAKES TOO MUCH ENERGY.

You have better things to do with your time. And won't you be disappointed when you discover what your friends already know—that you really are shallow. Think about all the blood, sweat, and tears—not to mention money—you'll save if you kiss introspection good-bye.

With all the money you've saved, book a cruise to some superficial, trendy, prefab resort.

SEPTEMBER 11 ∽

WHEN SOMEONE SAYS "NOTHING PERSONAL," IT'S PERSONAL.

Some people seem to think that somewhere in the unofficial rules of life, probably just after the No Backsies section, there's a line that says that you are allowed to say the most devastating things you can think of as long as you add the words *nothing personal*.

Reply, "How are your hemorrhoids, nothing personal."

SEPTEMBER 12 ∽

IT'S EASIER TO BE GLOOMY
THAN CHEERFUL.

Ain't that the truth. Between the high cost of health care, the lack of job security, and the continuing debate over which is deadlier, butter or margarine, what could you possibly be cheerful about? We expect such gloom in our lives that we've resorted to grasping at whatever straws we can to be cheerful: hot water for our morning shower, milk for our cereal, or a seat on the train. We're depressed just thinking about it.

Get a shoe shine or have your nails done.

SEPTEMBER 13 ∾

MAKING FUN OF OTHERS IS FUN.

Teasing and mocking the ugly, smelly, stupid, and socially challenged may not be politically correct, but it sure is a hoot. Being nice has its rewards, but we've never seen anybody fall on the floor laughing over a sincere compliment.

Be polite: only make fun of people behind their backs.

SEPTEMBER 14 ∾

NO ONE OR NO THING CAN HAVE POWER OVER THE WAY YOU FEEL—EXCEPT MAYBE YOUR EX-SPOUSE.

The divorce is final. You're a free person. You can get on with your life. Nothing can stop you now. Wait a minute. Is that the phone? Who could be calling at this hour? You pick up the receiver. It's your ex. You break out into a cold sweat. You start to shake. Suddenly you wake up. It's all been a bad dream.

Change your number.

SEPTEMBER 15 ∾

PEOPLE LIKE REVENGE.

People don't forget slights. They may have to wait years to get back at someone, but they'll get vengeance in the end. That's what fuels feuds. Any movie that shows a well-executed vendetta is bound to draw crowds.

Be kind; you never know when you'll need allies.

SEPTEMBER 16 ∾

YOU OWE MORE MONEY THAN YOU EARN.

It's the American way. You aren't truly American unless you're badly in debt. Savings? What the hell is that? You're busy trying to figure out where next month's rent or mortgage money is coming from.

Take out another loan.

SEPTEMBER 17 ⌒

STUFF WAITING TO BE RECYCLED ATTRACTS VERMIN.

Nowadays you're considered a moral degenerate if you don't recycle everything short of toilet paper. Before the debris is hauled off, most homes get to resembling the town dump. Even if you waste gallons of precious, pure water washing the cans and bottles, they still somehow retain enough "character" to attract bugs, flies, and rodents ranging from mice to raccoons.

Eat out more often.

SEPTEMBER 18 ∾

YOU WON'T BE ABLE TO PAY FOR
YOUR KID'S COLLEGE TUITION.

Got kids? Want them to go to something other than a trade school or some two-bit community college? Got $400,000? If you haven't been socking away at least $120 a month since the day your child was born, you can just forget it. Now your kid can't afford to go to college so she can kiss any job good-bye. No job, no money no place to live—except back home with you. Doesn't that sound fun?

Go out and buy something nice for yourself.

SEPTEMBER 19 ∽

YOUR CAR MAY HAVE BEEN
MADE ON A MONDAY.

People who work in auto plants say that cars made on Mondays are the worst. Lots of the assembly line workers are tired, hung over, and disinterested. Parts are screwed up or not screwed on. Cars made on Tuesdays after late Monday Night Football games are pretty bad, too. The only problem is, you have no way of knowing what day a car was made.

Know your state's lemon laws.

SEPTEMBER 20 ∽

FUR IS WARMER THAN SYNTHETICS.

It's a fact. Unfortunately, it's very politically incorrect right now. Most fur-wearing humans have to dodge frenzied animal lovers armed with cans of spray paint. You can eat meat, you just can't wear the pelt. Is there a double standard here, or what? Fur-bearing animals are natural and were put on this planet for a reason. Synthetics, on the other hand, are man-made and the factories that produce them create noxious chemicals as a by-product, which are then disposed of in our lakes and rivers rendering them unusable.

Layer.

SEPTEMBER 21 ∾

MOST PEOPLE BUY BOOKS TO DISPLAY THEM, NOT TO READ THEM.

We are a nation of literary lazybones (except for the wise, thoughtful readers of this book). For lots of people, books are the equivalent of silk flowers: nice, low-maintenance decorating accessories. And there are even fake books that are really cool boxes for hiding valuables.

Try books-on-tape. It's like reading without eye-strain.

SEPTEMBER 22 ∞

YOU'RE STILL COMPUTER ILLITERATE.

What are you waiting for? This is not another pet rock, yoyo, or hula hoop. Computers are here to stay. So you may as well stop fighting it and learn how the damn things work. If you don't, you can forget trying to communicate with anyone under the age of ten. Remember, today's kids are tomorrow's computer-dweeb, bureaucratic, you're-not-in-our-data-file distributors of our paltry Social Security checks and Medicaid benefits.

Move to Bali. Maybe computers haven't caught on there yet.

SEPTEMBER 23 ∽

MODERN ART IS A HOAX.

The perception that a child could be a modern artist is totally wrong. Sure, a kid or a chimp could create most of the work that's passed off as modern masterpieces. But they could never pull off the brooding, haughty, condescending inarticulateness that lures predatory dealers and charms insecure arrivistes.

Sign some junk with a made-up name and hang it on your wall. Almost no one will ever admit they don't get it.

SEPTEMBER 24 ∽

THERE'S A 50 PERCENT CHANCE
YOUR FIRST MARRIAGE
WILL END IN DIVORCE.

Married? You might not be for long. Thinking of getting married? You might want to think again. One in two marriages ends in divorce, and if you think that's depressing, 60 percent of all second marriages end in breakup. Not very happy odds.

If you're not married: when you do take the plunge, have one hell of a party and invite a lot of people so you get a lot of neat stuff. (*Hint*: don't forget to register someplace where you can turn in the gifts for cold, hard cash.) If you're already married: when you get married again, refer to the suggestion above.

SEPTEMBER 25 ∾

COCKROACHES WILL SURVIVE A
NUCLEAR BLAST, BUT HUMANS WON'T.

As a result of the Cold War scam, more than enough megatons to exterminate the human race are stockpiled all around the world. And some of those wonderful, automatic, strike-back mechanisms are probably still in place. So as soon as someone's elbow accidently hits a button, the human race will join the dinosaurs in the hall of fame of former planet rulers. Who will take over? Probably roaches. They are impervious to radiation.

Go further into debt; let the roaches deal with the trillion dollar deficit.

SEPTEMBER 26 ∽

IF YOU'RE EVER MUGGED, YOU WON'T FIGHT BACK.

You're a hero—in your mind. You've gone through all the scenarios: the two six-foot, six-inch thugs in the alley with the ice picks, the four nunchuk-wielding ninjas in the dimly lit parking lot, and the six Luger-toting Nazis in the vacant rathskeller bathroom. No problem. You're not alone. Many people have had those same fantasies. And even more people have been mugged and their dreams of retribution have been dashed. The odds are that you'll be mugged at least once in your life (especially if you live in an urban area) by some short, skinny, pock-marked drug addict with a rusted and bent Phillips head screwdriver. And you won't put up one bit of resistance. You'll be too freaked out. Sorry, that's what the statistics say.

Practice cowering in front of a mirror.

SEPTEMBER 27 ∽

MOST PEOPLE DON'T WASH AFTER GOING TO THE BATHROOM.

The chef, the waiter, the nurse, the masseur, the policeman searching you, the barber, the politician shaking your hand. Washing with soap and water is pretty basic, but lots of people just don't have the time, or don't want to deal with holding their dripping hands under a roaring reversed vacuum cleaner motor.

Try wearing gloves.

SEPTEMBER 28 ∽

PEOPLE DON'T LIKE TO GET INVOLVED.

We'll pass on this one, if you don't mind.
Talk to our lawyer.

SEPTEMBER 29 ∽

ONLY A FRACTION OF THE ELIGIBLE CITIZENS REGISTER AND VOTE.

Who wins almost every election? Mr. Apathy! Our country was founded to give everyone representation, and most of us couldn't care less.

Keep quiet. The fact that all those other people don't vote will make your vote more important—if you get around to voting.

SEPTEMBER 30 ∽

THE SAME THING THAT HAPPENED TO 78s, 45s, LPs, 8-TRACKS AND CASSETTES WILL HAPPEN TO CDS.

So you've accepted the fact that CDs are the medium of the future and started to collect them seriously. Already there are people in development labs creating the media of the future. Someday your precious CD collection will sit in an attic or basement gathering dust.

Hold off on buying the next Dr. Demento collection until it's on whatever comes after DAT.

OCTOBER 1 ∞

COMMERCIALS CAN MAKE YOU CRY.

You're a smart person. Surely you should be able to remain aloof and skeptical for thirty seconds. But somehow those tricky little demons on Madison Avenue always figure out how to get to you.

Channel surf during the commercials; make liberal use of the mute button.

OCTOBER 2 ∞

PRISONS MAKE BETTER CRIMINALS.

When we catch young criminals, we send them off to institutions where they get advanced training in crime from accomplished, veteran criminals.

Lock everything up.

OCTOBER 3 ∾

YOU NEVER KNEW THE REAL WORDS
TO "LOUIE, LOUIE."

It was your anthem of rebellion: dirty, nasty, raunchy. You loved it because your parents hated it. But it was all a juvenile gesture, because you never really knew what they were saying—you guessed, you nudged and winked, but you never knew. And now the song is considered mild enough to be featured at football games.

Forget the words: get a tape of the song, go for a drive, crank it up, and sing. Think of it as a long mantra.

OCTOBER 4 ∽

PEOPLE CAN LISTEN IN ON
YOUR CELLULAR CALLS.

It takes a warrant to tap a phone line, but it only takes a receiver to eavesdrop on a cellular phone. The endearments you whispered into your car phone really got some teenage techno-nerd excited. The business strategy discussion you had from your backyard was recorded and sold to your competitors. And the police have been tuning in to your portable ever since you dialed Montague and bought that gram of coke for old times' sake at the college reunion.

Use code names; it's fun.

OCTOBER 5 ∽

WE HAVE NO IDEA OF WHAT WE'RE DOING WITH NUCLEAR POWER.

Scientists confidently estimate half-lives of 50,000 years, give or take 20,000, knowing they'll be dead in 50 and will never be held accountable. Plants and storage systems are built by the contractors who come in with the lowest bid. And accidents throughout the military and the nuclear industry are routinely hushed up, so we can't even learn from them. We'd have a better chance of calling up the devil and controlling him than we do of dealing with nuclear power.

If you doubt us, buy real estate near a nuke plant; it'll be cheap.

OCTOBER 6 ∽

YOU HAVE NO WAY OF KNOWING WHAT'S REALLY IN CHINESE FOOD.

Chinese food is great. It's tasty, it can be cheap, it's fun to share, and you can often get it delivered in convenient containers. But what the heck is in it? Sure, they sometimes tell you about the major ingredients. But there are always a few strange things that look like Martian body parts. Does *moo shu* really mean cow's shoe? Under what gum is sub-gum found?

Go with the flow: order any dish on a Chinese menu that's misspelled; it's usually the most exotic.

OCTOBER 7 ∾

LAWYERS LIE FOR A LIVING.

Ask lawyers if they lie for a living and they'll say, "Not guilty." What did you expect? That's what they tell their clients to say, even when they're caught red-handed. Besides, lie is a short word; lawyers like longer phrases like "fulfill my duty by making sure that my client has the most advantageous representation possible, including presenting selected details in a way that will . . ." (We'd go on, but we don't get to charge by the hour.)

Remember: *politician* is the future tense of *lawyer*.

OCTOBER 8 ∽

TELEVISION IS MEDIOCRE BECAUSE
THAT'S WHAT VIEWERS WANT.

Complain all you want about commercial TV, but bear this in mind: it's a near perfect democracy. More people watch TV than vote, and the shows that stay on the air represent the true feelings and values of middle America.

Write your congressperson; tell him or her you want legislation forcing the networks to bring back shows like *Gilligan's Island* and *The Brady Bunch*.

OCTOBER 9 ∽

COLUMBUS DIDN'T DISCOVER ANYTHING.

Columbus may be a hero to some slackers because he figured out how to get other people to pay him to travel, but forget the idea that he discovered America. If that's true, we discovered New York City. Sure, there were people here, but we choose not to count them.

Find an empty lot and claim it in the name of Spain, Italy, Portugal, or wherever you were born.

OCTOBER 10 ∾

YOUR CAT LITTER STINKS.

If you're one of the millions of cat owners who operates under the delusion that your cat litter doesn't stink, think again. All cat litter stinks. The average cat emits more noxious fumes and by-products than the average paper plant. You just can't smell it any- more because your smell sensors have been perma- nently cauterized.

Train your cat to use the toilet like the rest of us.

OCTOBER 11 ∾

WHEN SOMEONE SAYS, "TO BE HONEST . . ." IT MEANS HE OR SHE NORMALLY ISN'T.

Think about it: someone has been "sharing" with you for twenty minutes, and they suddenly start a sentence with "To be honest . . ." or "To tell the truth . . ." or "Let me be straight with you." Doesn't that mean that all the rest of the stuff they've said was pure crap?

Embroider "To Be Honest . . ." on a throw pillow.

OCTOBER 12 ∽

PETER PAN WAS A CROSS-DRESSER.

It's bad enough that one of our children's major role models hated the concept of aging and maturing; we had to add to their confusion by letting females play the role. By the way, how many boys do you know who want to be Peter Pan when they grow up? Quite the dilemma, hey? While we're at it, why are we even discussing a play that vilifies a captain for an unfortunate deformity and focuses on his prosthesis rather than his character?

Think lovely thoughts.

OCTOBER 13 ∽

PRO WRESTLING IS FAKE.

Thought we'd mention this in case any of you hadn't caught on. What does our tolerance of this pointless charade say about our culture? Why is it so attractive to teenage boys? Then again, shouldn't we admire men willing to break sexual stereotypes by parading around in tights?

See October 12—Peter Pan Was a Cross-Dresser.

OCTOBER 14 ∾

YOU NEVER GET TO DRIVE
YOUR CAR AT TOP SPEED.

Your car was engineered to go 90, 100, 120, or maybe even 140 miles per hour. You paid for all that power, but you never get to use it because of all our restrictive speed limits.

Visit Germany and drive the autobahn; it'll cure you of the desire to drive fast.

OCTOBER 15 ∾

YOU LOOK BETTER WITH YOUR CLOTHES ON.

Face it, clothes serve an aesthetic purpose. They cover over the sag in your belly, the hairs on your butt, and the moles on your thighs, and they give people a fabric that's generally more pleasant to look at than your sweaty, mottled skin.

Make love in the dark.

OCTOBER 16 ∾

A PENNY SAVED IS MEANINGLESS.

Long ago, Ben Franklin made his reputation by telling people that "a penny saved is a penny earned." Pennies were more valuable back then and the standards for really good quips were a lot lower. Nowadays, a penny is less than worthless; it's a nuisance. And if you're all that worried about pennies, you're missing the big picture.

Collect currency with Franklin's picture on it instead.

OCTOBER 17 ∾

BE OPEN AND FRIENDLY TO THE WORLD AND PEOPLE WILL TAKE ADVANTAGE OF YOU.

It's a dog-eat-dog world. If you decide to be kind and gentle to your fellow humans, they'll take advantage of you in a heartbeat.

Buy a box of chocolates. People are like chocolates; some are cherries and some are nuts.

OCTOBER 18 ∽

NEVER DRAW TO FILL
AN INSIDE STRAIGHT.

We have no idea what this really means, but it goes to show that there are people out there who do. A number of people out there have done a lot of thinking about cards and how they're played. From what we've surmised, it has something to do with guys named Doc who sport pencil-thin moustaches and can make nickels come out of your ears.

Never play with money you're not ready to lose.

OCTOBER 19 ∽

WHEN SOMEONE SAYS,
"I'M NOT GOOD ENOUGH FOR YOU,"
HE OR SHE IS RIGHT.

If someone utters the above statement to you, it means one of two things. If you're breaking up, it's just a cheap trick to try and transfer the responsibility for the relationship's failure to you. If you're staying together, it means your partner has a dangerously low self-image. In either case, they don't really mean it, but they are right.

Don't be a fool. Don't argue.

OCTOBER 20 ∽

PAYBACKS ARE A BITCH.

Before you do people wrong, bear in mind that they will try to even the score. And when they get you back, you'll feel all the worse because you'll know you had it coming.

Follow the Golden Rule; it's hokey, but it could keep you from getting ambushed.

OCTOBER 21 ∽

YOUR BEST SURVIVAL SKILL IS SUBMISSION.

You're a survivor, right? What that means is that when the going gets tough, you bend over and assume the position.

You agree, don't you? Say, "yes." Louder! We can't hear you.

OCTOBER 22 ∽

EVEN IF YOU CAN'T SEE THE MARKUP, IT'S IN THERE.

Car dealers really started this game: they sell you something at their ticket price, but they don't tell you about the volume discount they get from the manufacturer at the end of the season. Businesses sell you stuff for what they paid for it, but don't mention that they bought it from a subsidiary at an inflated price. The book club sounds great, until you learn that they charge you four dollars for packing each book they send to you.

Tell them you believe it's unethical for you to take advantage of their offer; you only like situations where everyone wins.

OCTOBER 23 ∽

PEOPLE NOTICE IT WHEN YOU FART.

You think you get away with all those silent emissions? Think again. People notice, but are too decent to mention it, much less call you Pooter to your face. And you'll fart even more as you get older.

Get a dog. It's easy to blame a dog.

OCTOBER 24 ∽

IF IT'S "TOO GOOD TO BE TRUE," IT'S FALSE.

If the pay is high, it means the client is a monster. If the price is low, the car's a lemon. If the price is really low, there's no warranty. If the person at the other end of the bar is more gorgeous than anyone you have a right to be seen with, you're drunk or you're flirting with a hooker.

Remember to tell yourself, "I told you so," after you're seduced and out of cash.

OCTOBER 25 ∞

SOMEONE ELSE ALWAYS GETS THE CREDIT.

If you win at sports, your coach and trainer will take a bow. If you ship an enormous order on time, your boss will compliment the shippers. If you're a nice guy, people will compliment your parents. Even if you sign every page, painting, and sculpture you create, people will pop up, taking credit for being your teachers, guides, influences, and mentors.

Since they are willing to share the credit, feel free to share blame with them when you screw up.

OCTOBER 26 ∞

YOU FORGOT TO FLOSS.

If you don't floss, you'll never keep your teeth. But flossing is essentially disgusting. You try and cram both hands into your mouth and fish out rancid food bits from between your teeth with a spit-and-blood-soaked thread. No wonder you "forget" so often.

Encourage yourself to floss by reminding yourself how much you dislike the smell of the dentist's gloves.

OCTOBER 27 ∽

YOU, TOO, WILL BE FORGOTTEN.

Unless they donated a library, had a statue made of them, or wrote a really good book, the people who lived a hundred years ago have been forgotten. And the ones who are now remembered will be forgotten in another hundred years. The same will happen to you.

Borrow money. As long as the debt's outstanding, you'll be remembered.

OCTOBER 28 ∽

FIRING PEOPLE IS CONSIDERED A SIGN OF GOOD MANAGEMENT.

Long ago, the sign of great management was how happy the employees were. A really good company took care of its people until they earned their gold watches and collected their pensions. Now, investors and analysts look for companies with managers who know how to keep the head count down, how to move out the old folks, and how to leverage all that money sitting around in the pension fund.

Update your resume.

OCTOBER 29 ∞

SOMETHING YOU WERE EXPOSED TO TEN YEARS AGO MAY CAUSE YOU TO DEVELOP CANCER TEN YEARS FROM NOW.

Even if you live the rest of your life drinking only pure water and breathing only filtered air, some sneaky biological time bomb from your past is waiting to take you out. Maybe the rock your grandfather sent you from Arizona was radioactive or the odorless cleaning agent they used at the office is a slow-acting carcinogen.

Live each day like your last: party!

OCTOBER 30 ∞

YOUR RELATIVES WILL BE OVERCHARGED FOR YOUR FUNERAL.

It's bad enough that you're going to have to die, without some opportunistic vultures going after the remains of your bank account. But there's almost no way to stop them from descending on the grieving with manipulative lines like, "Wouldn't this silk-lined model be more appropriate for his place in the community?" and "This brass and ebony design truly conveys your respect." They even have the balls to sell elaborate coffins for bodies that are about to be cremated.

Let it go. What do you care? You'll be dead.

OCTOBER 31 ∞

YOU'RE TOO OLD FOR HALLOWEEN.

Halloween is the one perfect holiday: kids get to dress up and eat candy! But you're too old for it. If you dressed up and went trick-or-treating, people would think you were a pervert or a juvenile delinquent and call the local police.

Have a scotch; it's one advantage to being a grown-up.

NOVEMBER 1 ∞

AN IDIOT WITH A GUN CAN STOP
A GREAT PERSON.

Any time a wonderful human being begins to inspire people, there's always the possibility that some loser will get a gun and kill her or him.

Avoid inspiring people.

NOVEMBER 2 ∾

CRIMINALS RESPOND TO HARSHER LAWS BY RESISTING ARREST MORE VIOLENTLY.

Conservatives across the country are screaming for harsher laws. We're supposed to get tough on criminals. But, when getting caught means forty years in the slammer, criminals are more likely to try and shoot their way out when they're cornered. And, with "three strikes and you're out," no one will ever want to plea bargain and our courts will be jammed.

Bank by mail.

NOVEMBER 3 ∾

YOU STEAL OFFICE SUPPLIES.

You think of yourself as basically honest, but when was the last time you bought pens, pads, and paper clips? It's not grand larceny, and it's easy to rationalize given all the work you do at home. But it is stealing.

Buy a pencil or two. They only cost about a buck, and it could make you feel a little less guilty.

NOVEMBER 4 ∾

RUST NEVER SLEEPS.

Metal. It's supposed to be the hardest stuff there is. But even metal corrodes. And wood rots. Colors fade. Oil dries. Your joints stiffen, your arteries close.

Consider renting instead of buying.

NOVEMBER 5 ∾

IT HURT YOU MORE THAN IT HURT THEM.

Not only did your parents physically harm you, they poured salt into your wounds with the cosmically lame claim that spanking you hurt them more than it hurt you. Maybe if you had tacks in your pants with the points facing outward, but otherwise . . .

Get your hands on a book of matches. Play with them.

NOVEMBER 6 ✎

TIES CUT OFF THE SUPPLY OF BLOOD
TO THE BRAIN.

Ties have no useful function. They are essentially neck tourniquets. As a general rule, the more a job requires you to wear a tie, the less they want you to think.

Try one of them thar Texas string ties. You'll look like a dork, but you'll lose fewer brain cells.

NOVEMBER 7 ∽

WHEN OPPORTUNITY KNOCKED, YOU WERE OUT PICKING UP YOUR DRY CLEANING.

Don't let it happen again. In our modern, service-oriented age, there's absolutely no reason for you to leave your home or apartment. You can get your food and videos delivered, and you can even get a good bottle of wine brought directly to your doorstep. You can work at home; plug in your modem, crank up the computer, and punch in your fax number. It's ideal and you'll always be around when good old opportunity finally shows up. Hey, you can get rid of your car and think of all the gas money you'll save. Mugging will be a thing of the past. No one can hurt you because you're safe at home—waiting.

Install call waiting in case "Opportunity" decides to call ahead.

NOVEMBER 8 ∾

MONEY IS COMPLICATED.

Interest. Deductibility. Inflation. Opportunity cost. Present value. Liquidity. Somewhere along the line, money got real complicated.

Hoard all you can; money may be complicated, but poverty sucks.

NOVEMBER 9 ∾

YOU'RE LOSING YOUR FLEXIBILITY.

Ever watch babies? They can bend every which way; little boys can hang upside down for an hour at a time, and little girls can wing both legs back and sit comfortably on the ground while playing jacks. But not you, not anymore. You're at an age where it's smart to do stretches before climbing a flight of stairs.

Get a Jacuzzi; they're great therapy and you're old enough now that you don't need a parent hanging around playing lifeguard.

NOVEMBER 10 ∞

YOU'RE LOSING YOUR FLEXIBILITY.

You're getting set in your ways, too. When was the last time you tried a new kind of food or experimented with a new sexual position?

Say up late and watch some trashy TV programs.

NOVEMBER 11 ∞

GERMS ARE GETTING STRONGER.

There's a vicious cycle going on. Germs strike, we develop medicines that wipe most of them out, but a few develop resistance to the medicine and start a new colony of supergerms. Essentially, we've created an accelerated selective breeding process to create killer germs.

Buy a helmet, a canteen, and a rifle; declare germ warfare.

NOVEMBER 12 ✍

IF IT WEREN'T TAX DEDUCTIBLE,
YOU'D GIVE EVEN LESS TO CHARITY.

It's not like you tithe or anything, but you give your share. But are you giving strictly out of the goodness of your heart, or does the fact that it's tax deductible enter into the equation?

Give a quarter to a panhandler. Don't declare it on your taxes.

NOVEMBER 13 ∞

HALF OF THE PEOPLE IN ANY ADULT ED. CLASS ARE THERE LOOKING FOR A DATE.

Visit any adult education center and take the pulse. The atmosphere is as desperate as a dockside bar at closing. See the woman wearing the killer heels in the etching class? She's hunting. And notice that Mr. Toupee has used his breath spray three times already. What's with all the makeup during the Saturday massage class? And see the regional manager slip the ring off his finger before Survey of Recent Cinema?

Kill two birds with one stone: Find a class on How to Flirt.

NOVEMBER 14 ∞

YOU RARELY GET WHAT YOU ASK FOR.

Remember that really neat red fire truck you wanted? You didn't get. it, did you? How about the pony? For that matter, when was the last time you got a burger the way you wanted it?

Pretend you're getting married and register at a store for the things you want.

NOVEMBER 15 ∽

IF YOU GET WHAT YOU WISH FOR,
YOU'LL BE DISAPPOINTED.

How many times a day do you say, "Boy, I really wish I could . . ."? And what would you do if what you wished for came true? "I wish I didn't have to go to work today." ZING. You stay home and you **still** get paid for the day. "I wish I knew where I was going." ZIP. You're suddenly a road atlas. And our favorite, "I wish I had a million dollars." ZINGO. No more money problems. Then again, how many times a day have you said, "I can't believe how stupid that was. I'm so embarrassed, I wish I were dead." Think about it.

Stop believing in genies. Mothers-in-law get wishes, too.

NOVEMBER 16 ∽

TQM IS THE DRUG OF CHOICE FOR
HALF OF TODAY'S EXECUTIVES.

If you don't know what TQM (Total Quality Management) is, consider yourself lucky. Basically, it's
EST for executives. (Don't know EST? You're even
luckier!) Execs take TQM and start believing that
quality is a commodity that can be managed.

Post signs that say "Are you making quality?" on
the inside of all the bathroom stall doors.

THE THIRTEENTH STEP IS ADMITTING
THE FIRST TWELVE WERE POINTLESS.

Self-help programs are likely to put people through a lockstep progression that sounds more like a Masonic ritual than a journey of self-discovery. But they never tell you about the last step, which involves telling yourself that you are in charge. All the malarkey about saying that you are controlled by a Higher Power isn't self-help, it's self-surrender.

Will your hand to move. See, it happened—you are in control!

NOVEMBER 18 ∞

YOUR FRIENDS KNEW YOUR
CLOTHES WERE OUT OF FASHION
SIX MONTHS BEFORE YOU DID.

A friend will tell you if you have a booger hanging from your nose, you have a piece of lettuce caught in your front teeth, or your fly is open, but will she tell you that dress you're wearing went out with Wilma Flintstone or those bell bottoms died with Jimi Hendrix? We bet not. Fashion is a very sensitive topic in this culture of conforming individualism; it's good to be unique, but it's not good to be very unique.

Hire a personal shopper.

NOVEMBER 19 ∞

IF YOU WERE A VEGETABLE,
YOU'D BE A LIMA BEAN.

Some people are colorful and spicy; they'd be peppers. Some are sweet and invite you to squeeze them; they'd be tomatoes. Some have appeal; they're potatoes. You, on the other hand, would be a lima bean.

Choose a new favorite color.

NOVEMBER 20 ∞

YOU'D RATHER CHANGE OTHERS
THAN CHANGE YOURSELF.

We all know how difficult it is to make changes. Most of us are set in our ways and it's not a big secret that anything new is threatening. But how many friends or acquaintances do you know who would be better off if they just listened to the valuable advice you could give them; advice that could change them for the better? It would just take a minute. What's the big deal? You're not doing it for you, you're doing it for them. People can be so selfish sometimes.

Make a date with some friends and don't show up. That'll teach them they had better value your friendship.

NOVEMBER 21 ∾

NERDS RULE.

With the advent of technology, the chip is mightier than the fist. Now, the strong are those geeky techno-nerds who control the computers for banks, the military, and credit unions. They can make or break you with a tap of the key pad. Big Brother is here, and he's wearing taped glasses and a pocket protector.

Take a computer course. Learn their language.

NOVEMBER 22 ∾

YOU COULD HAVE DONE MORE.

Did you really give it your all or were you in too much of a hurry? People rely on you, but you have more important things to do. How could you be so selfish? You should be ashamed of yourself.

Whatever you're doing now, do more of it.

NOVEMBER 23 ∽

IF YOU'RE A TURKEY, YOU'LL GET EATEN.

It's the law of the jungle. The winners eat; the losers get stuffed and munched. Being nice doesn't work: look what happened to the Indians who helped the pilgrims.

Eat fast and be first in line for seconds. Take all the stuffing.

NOVEMBER 24 ∽

DIETS DON'T WORK.

Diets are our way of transferring our real guilts and feelings into something with calories. We will always feel guilt, we will forever go on diets that don't work.

Pig out on a box of Twinkies. Don't share them.

NOVEMBER 25 ∾

MEAT IS MURDER.

Most of us believe that devouring other species is part of the natural cycle of life. You really don't care that the venison on your plate was Bambi's second cousin once removed, or that lapin aux pommes and canard en croute call for the dead relatives of Bugs Bunny and Daffy Duck. The only difference between you and the Argentinean soccer players who ate each other after their plane crashed is that it's easier to get your hands on a Big Mac here than it is in the Andes.

Go to a petting zoo. Feel guilty.

NOVEMBER 26 ∾

TOFU SUCKS.

Just about every nonmeat diet relies on tofu. Fried tofu. Raw tofu. Tofu in soup. The only problem is that most packing materials have more taste than tofu. Don't ask us how we know.

Find out what tofu is. Let us know.

NOVEMBER 27 ✑

MANY CHURCHES HARBOR
ROBED CHILD MOLESTERS.

Some priests have a true calling; others just hear voices and like to wear dresses. And most churches' idea of forgiveness means that they forgive their own trespasses, so, after Father Oh'kneel is caught teaching the altar boys and girls to blow Gabriel's horn, he's given a vacation in the desert and sent to shepherd new lambs in an unsuspecting parish.

Teach your children to be suspicious of men who wear flats with dresses.

NOVEMBER 28 ∽

YOU'LL OUTLIVE THE PETS YOU LOVE.

This should be no big revelation to you pet lovers. If you're in your midthirties and grew up with pets, you've probably gone through three dogs or cats (average life expectancy twelve years), about seven rabbits (average life expectancy five years) or approximately nine guinea pigs (average life expectancy four years). Don't get caught by surprise (or denial), start making those funeral arrangements for Spot, Fluffy, Thumper, and Ramrod now.

Buy yourself a healthy Asian elephant; he or she has a maximum longevity of seventy-seven years. You can get old together and you only have to come up with one cute name.

NOVEMBER 29 ∽

YOU THINK THE INTERNET
IS A FISHING TERM.

You're probably one of those people who thinks http://cia.quote.com is a major typo or pfreebase@aol.com is the politically correct way of writing dirty words. Well, you're wrong. They're both e-mail addresses on the Internet. The Internet is the communication center of the next century. And where are you? Still on the phone or writing letters and sending them via snail mail? Get with the program. By the way, since the Internet isn't monitored so carefully, it's a great place to send and receive graphic pornography. (Try that on the phone or through the post office and you'll have the FCC or the Postmaster General on your butt.)

Spend two or three hours discovering that all the really good Internet names are taken.

NOVEMBER 30 ∞

DEEP DOWN INSIDE, YOU'D RATHER
STAY HOME WITH THE KIDS.

In this competitive day and age, there's no way you can be both an involved parent and a successful businessperson. You have to make a choice. Do you really want to work fourteen hours a day for peanuts while you put up with some idiot boss, or would you rather be with the kids playing in the park, reading fun stories, and taking naps? Okay, you might have to change a stinky diaper or two, pick creamed corn out of your hair, and say "no-no" a couple of million times, but at least you're the boss. And the return is better.

Go for it: stay home and take care of the kids. Instill enough guilt so the little tykes make sure to take care of you in your dotage.

DECEMBER 1 ∽

GO WITH YOUR GUT; ALWAYS LISTEN TO THE LARGEST PART OF YOUR BODY.

How often have you said, "Damn, I was going to say that!" or "I knew it! That was my first guess!"? It's happened more often than you want to remember, right? Instincts have been given a bad rap by our modern, empirical, you've-got-to-have-proof society. If the scientists had their way, intuition would be erased from our primordial memory banks. It's time to wake up and give credit to your natural impulses.

If you ever have to take a standardized test again in this life, don't study for it.

DECEMBER 2 ∾

YOU DON'T HAVE A CLUE AS
TO WHO YOU ARE.

What do you really, truly believe in? How would you describe yourself to a stranger? If you were an animal, what animal would that be? Stuck? No fair asking your friends for help. We're not surprised. You're so busy criticizing and appraising others that you don't have any time to check out your own self.

Buy a Ouija board and sit in a dark room.

DECEMBER 3 ∽

THANK-YOU NOTES SUCK.

You're invited over to someone's house for dinner so you've got to get dressed up, bring a bottle of wine or a bunch of flowers, and pretend to like whatever swill is being served. And for all this aggravation you're supposed to write a thank-you note. What about that really ugly vase you got on your birthday from your Aunt Gertrude? That's right, another thank-you note. What a waste of time and postage, especially if you had a lousy time or really hate the gift.

If you feel you really must thank your host or gift giver, wait until you're at work and phone him or her. May as well do it on the company's time and let them pay for the call.

DECEMBER 4 ∞

DOGS AREN'T SMART AND FAITHFUL, THEY'RE STUPID.

Lassie, Rin Tin Tin, Asta, Benji, Scooby Doo, and the rest of those mutts are tools of the media. Books, movies, and cartoons have anthropomorphized dumb dogs into caring, feeling, faithful, humanlike entities. What a bunch of dog doo. Ever watch *Lassie?* "Lassie," pleads June Lockhart as she tries to free her foot from the bear trap she stupidly stepped into, "go back to the house. The red bear trap remover is on the kitchen counter by the refrigerator. Bring it back to me. And hurry!" Lassie tears twenty miles back to the house, goes into the kitchen, and jumps up on the counter. The mutt grabs the tool in her mouth and charges back to June. "Lassie, good girl . . . Oh, that's not the red bear trap remover, that's the green badger trap remover. Go back and try it again. I really don't want to have to gnaw my foot off." Come on, one-word commands are the extent of a dog's mental ability. Dogs aren't the only stupid ones. (Fun Facts: dogs are color-blind, and there was more than one Lassie.)

Refuse to watch any show starring a dog—or for that matter starring any animal—except *Flipper*. Now, that was one smart pet.

DECEMBER 5 ∾

HALF OF ALL SURGERY IS UNNECESSARY.

Fads come and go. For a while, kids collected baseball cards, then they switched to Power Rangers. Now Pogs are all the rage. Surgery is just as capricious. For a while doctors liked to cut out tonsils, then they moved on to hysterectomies. Now the triple bypass is popular. And most studies show about half of these operations were unnecessary.

Get a second opinion.

DECEMBER 6 ∾

THE ARMY GIVES WEAPONS
TO LOSERS WHO THINK BEING
IN THE ARMY IS A STEP UP.

Imagine that society has treated you so badly that crewcuts, 5:30 A.M. marches, and group bathrooms without stalls seem attractive. Or maybe joining up was a preferable option to serving time for that assault charge. And now you're given all sorts of weapons. What would you do?

Camouflage your house.

DECEMBER 7 ∽

ANY FRUITCAKE YOU GET IS LIKELY TO BE AT LEAST SIX YEARS OLD.

Think it's nice that old Aunt Charlotte thought to send you a treat? Before you dig in, consider the fact that fruitcakes have a longer shelf life than rocks, and that most people treat fruitcakes as some sort of food-based chain letter. No telling what's festering in that thing. Come to think of it, Aunt Charlotte never did like you.

String it up outside, see if the crows and raccoons will go near it.

DECEMBER 8 ∽

YOUR TEENAGE CHILDREN AND
THEIR FRIENDS LAUGH AT
YOU BEHIND YOUR BACK.

You are never going to be hip to either your children or their friends. Any attempts at being cool in front of your kids will be met with embarrassment (yours and theirs). Part of your child's rite of passage is the belief that his parents are complete jerks. We don't care if you sport a ponytail, wear an earring, or have a cute little heart tattoo on your butt—you're still going to be labeled a member of the establishment.

Live long enough so you can hear their kids laugh at them.

DECEMBER 9 ∽

SOME PEOPLE SLEEP THEIR
WAY TO THE TOP.

There are all sorts of ways to get ahead. While it'd be nice to believe that the system is a strict meritocracy, some people get their promotions by lying and laying. And there's nothing you can put in a memo or a performance report that will match the power of an innuendo whispered across a pillow.

Keep your eyes open. If you're lucky enough to discover one of these office trysts, use it to your advantage. (Hint: special "gifts" in the form of money or promotions to quell those pesky threats of injurious revelation usually work for us.)

DECEMBER 10 ∞

THE STARS WHO TURN YOU ON ARE YOUNG ENOUGH TO BE YOUR CHILDREN.

The bods and bimbos in bikinis on *Baywatch*, *Beverly Hills 90210*, and *Melrose Place* are all about twenty years old. They've never seen a record and the Vietnam War is ancient history to them.

Reread *Lolita*.

DECEMBER 11 ∞

THE UNITED STATES IS NO LONGER DOMINANT.

The U.S. may be "the only remaining superpower," but it's like being the last remaining buggy whip factory. Certainly the Serbs and Croats don't stop fighting when we say so. South American drug lords thumb their noses at us. African warlords easily elude our army. Asian countries feel free to cane our citizens.

Proclaim yourself a sovereign nation. Declare war on the U.S., lose, and demand reparation to the tune of $100,000,000.

DECEMBER 12 ∞

MAKING LOVE WHILE LISTENING TO YOUR INNER CHILD IS JUST ANOTHER FORM OF SEX ABUSE.

Gross us out. Please tell us you don't do it until after your inner child is safely tucked into bed. You could go to jail if you're caught fooling around while your inner child is still in the room. Do you want to warp the kid for the rest of its life?

Find a support group. Abstain from sex. Take up needlepoint.

DECEMBER 13 ∞

IF YOU HAD BEEN A PIONEER, THE INDIANS WOULD STILL RULE.

It's fun to read about the pioneers but, face it, you have no clue as to how to hunt or farm or tan or churn or forge or scout. You are not an explorer. The thought of living without indoor plumbing makes you break out in a cold sweat.

Rev up the microwave.

DECEMBER 14 ❧

THE WOODSTOCK GENERATION
SOLD OUT.

All that peace and love stuff went by the wayside when we got a little older; we decided we wanted our own stuff, we didn't want to share, and mine is bigger than yours.

Eat a pint of Cherry Garcia or Wavy Gravy while watching Woodstock II on Pay Per View. Use the big-screen TV in the media room.

DECEMBER 15 ❧

THE WORLD IS NOT FAIR.

You don't always get rewarded for hard work. Cheaters often win (*see June 9—Cheaters Prosper*). Bad things happen to good people.

Find a frail three-year-old and challenge her to an arm wrestling match.

DECEMBER 16 ∞

SEXUALLY TRANSMITTED DISEASES.

Need we elaborate? Free love will never happen again. The permissive '60s and '70s are over.

Call your college roommate, say you want your Henry Miller and Anaïs Nin books back.

DECEMBER 17 ∞

CHANGE IS AS LIKELY TO MAKE
THINGS WORSE AS TO IMPROVE THEM.

Thinking about changing? Just remember that different isn't necessarily better. Things can always get worse.

Change your underwear. That's about the only positive change we can think of.

DECEMBER 18 ∽

YOU DON'T REALLY LIKE FOREIGN MOVIES.

Admit it. As soon as you hear the words "foreign movie," you think "reading." And reading means work. Reading also means your friends—or worse yet, that first date you're trying to impress—will tell by your response time how slow a reader you really are. This is especially embarrassing when you're the only one not laughing two seconds after some particularly witty Peruvian bon mot translated into English appears on the screen.

Take a speed reading course or claim to suffer from "night blindness."

DECEMBER 19 ∽

YOUR CHILDHOOD IS OVER—YOU CAN'T FIX IT.

Don't buy all that hooey about fixing your life by delving into your past and reliving the incident when you were three and wet the bed. It's over.

Cancel your next three therapy sessions.

DECEMBER 20 ∞

MOST OF THE HOLIDAY CARDS YOU GET ARE FROM BUSINESSES.

Remember when you wished you would get more Christmas cards? Now you do. But take a good look at them; they're from the bank, the insurance guy, your dentist, and the Chinese restaurant. People don't care about you—they want your money.

Open the window and shout, "Bah, humbug."

DECEMBER 21 ∞

"CODEPENDENCE" SHOULD ONLY BE USED TO DESCRIBE SIAMESE TWINS.

We are each independent. We are each accountable for the idiotic things that we do. You do not control the people around you. They do their own wacko things without any help or approval from you.

Repeat after me: "I am an individual. I have my own thoughts, wishes, and desires." Come on, you in the back row, I can't hear you.

DECEMBER 22 ∽

WHEN SOMEONE SAYS,
"IT'S AS GOOD AS NEW," IT'S NOT.

Good as new is a euphemism. Cars, cameras, and houses are just like virgins—either they're new or they're used.

Bargain hard.

DECEMBER 23 ∽

A STITCH IN TIME MEANS
IT'S NO LONGER NEW.

A stitch in time may save the whatever from developing a nine-inch rip, but it still means that the darn thing is coming apart.

Let it rip and look punk.

DECEMBER 24 ∞

THERE IS NO SANTA CLAUS.

There it is again, that harsh reality—your parents lied to you. What's worse, you were dumb enough to believe that some tremendously fat guy was going to fit down your chimney.

Light a fire in the fireplace on Christmas Eve, just in case.

DECEMBER 25 ∞

HOLIDAYS ARE A BUMMER.

Know any shrinks? Ask them about this time of year. They'll tell you that almost everyone out there has some problem with holidays. Folks remember the wonderful family that's now gone or they remember that they never had a wonderful family like the ones in the holiday movies. All your holiday merriment is just an incredibly forced attempt to appear happy.

Don't wait—open your presents now.

DECEMBER 26 ∽

THE ONLY WAY TO WIN THE LIFE
INSURANCE GAME IS TO DIE YOUNG.

Talk about a no-win proposition. You live a long time, the insurance company gets a lot of your money. You die young, they pay someone you love—but you're still dead!

Talk your relatives into making *you* the beneficiary on *their* policies.

DECEMBER 27 ⁓

YOU WERE PROBABLY ADOPTED.

How do you know your parents are really your parents? You may look like them, but that doesn't mean anything. (How many times have you seen dogs that look exactly like their masters?) Maybe you're really adopted and your foster parents took you in because they felt sorry for you. This means you had better be on your best behavior because they can trade you in for a better child. (No, it doesn't matter how old you are.) The adoption service could be trying to reach your fake parents right now with the name of your replacement.

Monitor all mail and phone calls.

DECEMBER 28 ∽

OUR SOCIETY RUNS ON
GUILT AND REPRESSION.

Get rid of all guilt and repression? Heaven forbid.
Without those controls, that really big guy who lives
down the block would be having a great time raping
you, your mother, and your sister.

Put some extra locks on the doors.

DECEMBER 29 ∽

SOMEONE YOUNGER THAN YOU IS
WILLING TO DO YOUR JOB FOR LESS.

You need your job to pay your bills. But someone
a bit younger, maybe even someone who is still living
at home for free, would be happy to have your job,
even if it paid a little less than you make.

Whenever possible, make your job sound as difficult as possible.

258

DECEMBER 30 ∾

YOU THINK WITH YOUR GENITALIA.

They say two heads are better than one. And since the one head is jam-packed with ideas, thoughts, practical stuff, and details, boys let the other head do all the emotional thinking for them. Girls think with the second head they wish they had. Okay, our genitals do get us in trouble from time to time, but hey, we're only human.

Pamper yourself. Buy some satin underwear.

DECEMBER 31 ∾

COFFEE IS A DRUG.

Coffee is so addictive that people in countries too poor to afford plumbing spend their meager funds on it. Brave souls who try to give up this habit suffer horrible withdrawal headaches. Pregnant women are advised to stop drinking it. And if that's not enough to put any sane individual off the stuff, it can stain your teeth permanently.

Wake up and smell the coffee—but don't drink the stuff.

Do you have any doses of reality we neglected to mention? We'd like to hear from you. Please send them to:

WAKE UP AND SMELL THE COFFEE
The Berkley Publishing Group
200 Madison Avenue
New York, NY 10016

We're sorry, but no compensation or credit can be given. That's reality.

Andrew Frothingham and **Tripp Evans** have written a number of humor and reference books together. Some of the titles include: *Well-Done Roasts, Crisp Toasts, Creative Excuses for Every Occasion: Old Standards, Innovative Evasions and Blaming the Dog,* and *And I Quote* (coauthor Ashton Applewhite). Both reside in New York City.

Andrew Frothingham, a member of the Authors Guild, became an author and speechwriter after earning two Harvard degrees and surviving careers in advertising, real estate, carpentry, research, and education.

Tripp Evans is the author of *Normal Men, Desperate Women* (a takeoff on the self-help movement), coauthor of a popular joke book series, and has written a number of young adult books. He has earned his master of social work degree and is currently a practicing psychotherapist in New York City.